Words of Life

The Bible Day by Day
September–December 2009

HODDER &
STOUGHTON

First published in Great Britain in 2009 by Hodder & Stoughton
An Hachette Livre UK company

1

A CIP catalogue record for this title is available from the British Library

ISBN 978 0 340 97939 6

Typeset in Minion by Avon DataSet Ltd, Bidford on Avon, Warwickshire

Printed and bound in Great Britain
by Clays Ltd, St Ives plc

Hodder & Stoughton policy is to use papers that are natural, renewable
and recyclable products and made from wood grown in sustainable forests.
The logging and manufacturing processes are expected to conform to the
environmental regulations of the country of origin.

Hodder & Stoughton Ltd
338 Euston Road
London NW1 3BH

www.hodderfaith.com

Contents

Returning to Matthew's Gospel

28–31 December

Sundays

Most of the Sunday readings continue a *Words of Life* pattern, employing verse.

From the writer of *Words of Life*

Lyrics of the lilting song 'Try to remember' advise: 'Try to remember and if you remember, then follow.' '*If*' can be the issue. Aside from the brain diseases that increasingly affect millions of the aged around the world, everyone experiences an occasional lapse of memory. We're offered numerous ways to stimulate our minds and prevent memory loss.

Scripture abounds with verses that call God's people to remember him and his goodness. At times they record that his people forgot him and their hearts needed memory prompts. But God does not forget his promises, his covenant or his people.

This edition of *Words of Life* contains spiritual memory-prompts from Abraham's life, Jude's instruction, Matthew's record of Jesus' ministry, Paul's letter to the Colossians and Isaiah's prophecy. We also consider selected Scripture from some memorial markers.

Visuals can aid memory. In her Advent adventures Major Rachel Tickner tells of two incidents when art intersected with life and served to amplify the truth of Scripture in memorable ways.

Another aid to memory is repetition. We see Abraham and Sarah relearning lessons and returning to places of previous blessing to renew vows to God. For the Sunday readings, hymnwriters, poets and psalmists aid our hearts as we worship the Lord and remember his holy day. We might read their words more than once or aloud.

The word 'remember' from Latin and French origins is a fourteenth-century word meaning to be mindful again. The women at Jesus' tomb on the first Easter understood that meaning when the angels told them to remember that Jesus had told them he would be crucified and then raised on the third day. When they remembered his words they had an 'aha!' moment (Luke 24:6–8). What Jesus had said finally made sense to them.

We can have 'aha!' moments of discovery as we ask the Holy Spirit to help us. When the Bible is read, studied, taught or preached, Christ speaks; and when Jesus speaks, he brings life out of death. Then the Scripture is life-giving and life-transforming.

Jesus said: 'But the Counsellor, the Holy Spirit, whom the Father will send in my name, will teach you all things and will *remind* you of everything I have said to you' (John 14:26). Those are the things we most need to remember. May it be so for each of us as we follow Christ.

Evelyn Merriam
New York, USA

Abbreviations

AB   The Amplified Bible. Copyright © 1965 Zondervan.

ABNT   The Anchor Bible New Translation. © 1993 Doubleday.

ASV   The American Standard Version.

CEV   Contemporary English Version.

ESV   English Standard Version.

JBP   *The New Testament in Modern English*, J. B. Phillips © J. B. Phillips, 1958, 1959, 1960, 1972. HarperCollins Publishers.

JMT   James Moffatt Translation. © 1922, 1924, 1925, 1926, 1935. HarperCollins Publishers.

KJV   King James Bible (Authorised Version).

MSG   *The Message*, Eugene H. Peterson. © 1993, 1994, 1995, 1996, 2000, 2001, 2002. Used by permission of NavPress Publishing Group.

NASB   New American Standard Bible. © 1995.

NCV   New Century Version.

NKJV   New King James Bible®. Copyright © 1982 by Thomas Nelson, Inc. Used by permission. All rights reserved.

NLT   New Living Translation. © Tyndale House Publishers, 1996, 1998.

NRSV   New Revised Standard Version.

RSV   Revised Standard Version.

SASB   *The Song Book of The Salvation Army*. Copyright © 1986 The General of The Salvation Army.

WNT   Weymouth New Testament.

Something Beautiful, Something Good

Introduction

When we finished discussing Genesis back in February, Abram had responded to God's call. We return to Genesis in chapter 12 and will go through chapter 24 (the Easter 2003 and 2005 editions commented on the greater portion of the second half of Genesis, chapters 25–50).

Abram and Sarai receive new covenant names. We continue to learn from their pilgrimage of faith. The couple has to be taught some lessons more than once before they grasp their relevance or importance. But by God's grace and mercy they do learn.

A poem by Antonio Machado, translated from Spanish by Robert Bly, comes to mind:

> Last night, as I was sleeping
> I dreamt – marvellous error! –
> that I had a beehive
> here inside my heart.
> And the golden bees
> were making white combs
> and sweet honey
> from my old failures.

We see Abraham taking an active role with neighbouring tribes and cities as a concerned resident of the area. We listen as he intervenes on Lot's behalf when the LORD reveals his intention to destroy Sodom after its multifaceted sins shrieked for heaven's judgment. We delight in the long-awaited promised son's arrival. We see Abraham sometimes obeying God's direction right away – setting to the task early the next day. We watch him pass an incredible test of trust, grieve for his beloved wife, plan for Isaac's future and finally die at the 'good old age' of 175.

Abraham could have sung Gloria Gaither's chorus:

> Something beautiful, something good;
> All my confusion he understood.
> All I had to offer him
> Was brokenness and strife,
> But he made something beautiful of my life.

But we start with a detour to Egypt . . .

Off to Egypt

*'Now there was a famine in the land, and Abram went down to Egypt
to live there for a while because the famine was severe' (v. 10).*

We may lose track of time in an all-consuming task, but our stomachs remind us when it's meal time. Even potential hunger can motivate. The area where Abram stopped temporarily had a famine, so he decided to seek food and sanctuary for his entourage.

Others would do the same. Sometimes in Scripture famine was foretold. Amos even foretold a famine of hearing words of the Lord (Amos 8:11). When Joseph interpreted the Pharaoh's dreams and predicted seven years of plenty and seven of famine, he was able to put a plan in place to feed the Egyptians. Ultimately God used the plan to save Joseph's family and bring them to Egypt.

When Elisha advised the Shunammite widow to escape famine, she and her son lived in Philistia for seven years. Elimelech and Naomi moved with their sons from Bethlehem to Moab to escape famine. During a famine Isaac moved his family to Philistia when God warned him not to go to Egypt.

But the famine of Abram's time is the first recorded in the Bible. Did it make him wonder why God had brought him to Canaan? His decision to head for the well-watered delta of Egypt 'for a while' seemed logical. As they entered Egypt he worried about his safety. In fear he conspired with his beautiful wife to deceive the authorities and protect himself with a half truth.

Abram failed to keep the bigger picture in view. Yet because of God's intervention, Pharaoh discerned the true situation. Sarai was kept from harm. However, Pharaoh's favourable treatment of Abram ended abruptly and he deported the company in dishonour.

When food shortages and escalating prices cause riots, we can understand how a crisis such as a famine could cause a man to compromise his moral values and doubt God's providential care. In advance we pray with the hymnwriter, Frances Ridley Havergal:

> I am trusting thee, Lord Jesus,
> Never let me fall;
> I am trusting thee for ever,
> And for all.

Back to Bethel

'From the Negev he went from place to place until he came to Bethel,
to the place between Bethel and Ai where his tent had been earlier
and where he had first built an altar. There Abram called on the
name of the LORD' (vv. 3, 4).

In spite of his growing wealth in livestock and precious metals, Abram must have returned to Bethel humbled. He passed through the region where he had been when he'd decided to go to Egypt and returned to the place where he had first built an altar – Bethel ('house of God'). We sometimes need to return to the place of earlier basic spiritual commitments to renew our vows and seek a fresh blessing from God.

When Abram's and Lot's herdsmen quarrelled over pasture land, it seemed impractical to keep them vying for the same resources. Abram reminded Lot that they were relatives and spoke against such quarrelling or contention (*merbah*). Years later the Israelites in the wilderness complained to Moses and doubted God. The place where God provided water was called Meribah ('contention').

Did Abram's recent humiliation in Egypt embolden his nephew, Lot, to choose the well-watered land (like that of Egypt)? Or did Abram's hard lesson keep Abram from asserting his land rights as elder head of the clan? Abram must have thought their common bond worth saving. Perhaps Abram's magnanimity toward Lot in giving the younger man a choice of what was actually all Abram's was a testimony to Abram's refreshed faith in God and his promises.

Lot's choice revealed something of his nature as one's choices do. His choice would lead him to set up camp near Sodom. What appealed to him in the short term was not good for him over time. What he thought was more would be much less. In the end, he was mistaken. Spiritual wealth outweighs material possessions. As followers of Christ, we seek the Holy Spirit's guidance and wisdom in our choices. We pray with songwriter Harry Anderson:

> I want thy wisdom from above
> That I thy perfect way may see;
> To follow thee unblamable,
> Live thou thy life in me.
> (*SASB* 455)

To Hebron

*'So Abram moved his tents and went to live near the great trees of
Mamre at Hebron, where he built an altar to the LORD' (v. 18).*

When Lot heads east, Abram is left with God who tells him to look at and then
walk through the land of promise. God says that he will give Abram and his
descendants all the land he can see in every direction and the land grant will be for
ever.

Does childless Abram wonder more about the perpetual deed of land or the
descendants? God reassures him that he will have innumerable descendants who
will continue to inherit it all. This conversation probably took place during
daylight since God refers to the dust of the earth which Abram can see.

Lot had looked over the land and chosen a location he thought best for him.
Now God tells Abram to look in all directions at the land he will give him. Abram
leaves his choice with the God he trusts. Better to wait for God's gift than select
our own.

In his journey of faith Abram is learning the value of God's promises. God's
Word is the testament or will of our inheritance. Trusting God's provision loosens
our grip on our possessions. A Christian finance counsellor said that the first step
a believer should take to straighten out his finances is to be generous. It implies
awareness of true value.

Now that Abram has looked in all directions, God invites him to walk through
the land and see it for himself. So Abram travels about, and settles at Hebron, then
known as Mamre, near its great terebinth trees. These may have been oak-like trees
with thick boughs offering shade. The towering trees must have been remarkable.

Other places in Scripture mention such trees as locations sometimes favoured
for pagan worship (Hosea 4:13). But here in the choice setting Abram builds an
altar to Yahweh. This was the third place where he built an altar and worshipped
God. The first at Shechem was in response to God's promise; the second at Bethel
was a place to call on the name of the Lord (Genesis 12:6–8). Abram's altar at
Hebron may have been in gratitude for God's gracious promise.

Altars are vital. Old Testament altar-building may have inspired Samuel
Brengle, who advised us to carry an altar in our heart.

To Battle

*'And blessed be God Most High, who delivered your enemies
into your hand' (v. 20).*

Chapter 14 shows Abram in a different light from other passages. We see him as an astounding champion general.

Five kings of city-states just south of the Dead Sea which had been subject to another king for twelve years finally rebelled against the tyrant. After he gathered allies and warred against the five plus a whole territory in the area, the five city-state kings drew up battle lines against their foe in a valley full of tar pits. When two of the city-state kings fled, some of their soldiers fell into the pits. The rest fled to the hills. This gave the foe opportunity to invade and plunder their cities, Sodom and Gomorrah. Abram's nephew, Lot, who had moved into Sodom, was among those abducted.

When Abram hears about his nephew's plight, he is drawn to the conflict. By this time he has established a mutual protection confederacy with three neighbouring heads of clans in the peaceful Hebron area. Abram organises some of his trained men and with the allies of the confederacy attacks the four marauding kings and their forces at night. He successfully routs them. He rescues Lot and his possessions, brings back the women and others and recovers all the plundered goods.

Abram the victor is met by the kings of Salem and Sodom. One offers him blessing, the other a deal. King Melchizedek attributes the victory to God and a sign of God's approval of the patriarch. Abram discerns Melchizedek's spiritual stature and not only receives his blessing but pays him one tenth of all he has. (This is the first reference to giving a tithe in the Bible.)

King Bera offers Abram the booty of the conquest but wants his people of Sodom returned. Abram wisely declines any share for himself, wanting just what belongs to those who fought with him. Freedom comes from not hoarding the benefits of serving God.

Faith in and obedience to God are still prerequisites for victory. In the New Testament we read that a believer's battles are spiritual. God calls his Christian soldiers to own and hone weapons for spiritual warfare (Ephesians 6). Are we ready?

At Night

'After this, the word of the LORD came to Abram in a vision: "Do not be afraid, Abram. I am your shield, your very great reward"' (v. 1).

A bram has exhibited skill in organising his servants and neighbours, courage and concern in routing the invaders and rescuing Lot. He has shown wisdom in his dealings with the two very different kings. Now 'after this' – after the adrenalin surge of the pursuit, the victory, the royal meetings – the word of the Lord comes to him with reassurance in a vision.

We know the exhaustion that can follow exhilaration of any kind. And this encounter happens at night – just the time for doubts. Is Abram (who was first called 'the Hebrew' or 'one who came from beyond' in Genesis 14) feeling like an outsider, a misfit? Anyone who has lived immersed in another culture and language will identify with this.

Is he worried about the delay in seeing the fulfilment of God's promises to him? Does he wonder if his miss-steps in Egypt or his nephew's choice to move to Sodom have impinged on the promises? Is he concerned about the defeated kings returning in revenge? Does he have second thoughts about refusing to accept booty of war?

God anticipates Abram's needs and comes with words of encouragement: 'Don't be afraid, Abram. I'm your shield. Your reward will be grand!' (15:1, *MSG*). This is the first of many times in the Bible that the Lord or his messenger will say 'fear not' to someone. If it comes from God and is accompanied by his promised presence, protection and provision, as it is here, it is a strengthening command.

In this atmosphere of assurance Abram is able to voice his overarching question: what good is a reward to me since the heir to my estate is my servant from Damascus? The Lord counters Abram's deduction with a fact: your own son will be your heir.

To reinforce his point with a visual aid, God takes Abram outside and tells him to look at the night sky's innumerable stars and know that his offspring will also be innumerable. Abram believes God. Every clear night he will remember. What reminds you of God's promises and faithfulness? Let it prompt you to thank him.

You, of Abraham my Friend

But you, O Israel, my servant,
  Jacob, whom I have chosen,
  you descendants of Abraham my friend,
I took you from the ends of the earth,
  from its farthest corners I called you.
  I said, 'You are my servant';
  I have chosen you and have not rejected you.
So do not fear, for I am with you;
  do not be dismayed, for I am your God.
  I will strengthen you and help you;
  I will uphold you with my righteous right hand.

All who rage against you
  will surely be ashamed and disgraced;
  those who oppose you
  will be as nothing and perish.
Though you search for your enemies,
  you will not find them.
  Those who wage war against you
  will be as nothing at all.
For I am the LORD, your God,
  who takes hold of your right hand
  and says to you, Do not fear;
  I will help you.

Night Covenant

'On that day the LORD made a covenant with Abram and said,
"To your descendants I give this land"' (v. 18).

God reassured Abram about his heir and Abram believed him unreservedly. James 2:23 says that Abram's belief was counted as righteousness. Abram was learning to trust the Lord for things he couldn't do for himself. Our unreserved faith in Christ as Saviour does the same for us – puts us on the way of righteousness.

God added confirmation about bringing Abram to the land of promise. Abram inquired how he could know he'd possess it. Again God offered a visual aid, but this one required Abram's participation.

It was a dramatic covenant ritual known in the ancient world. Sacrificed animals were cut into pieces and those making a covenant walked between the parts as if to say, we'd rather be torn apart than break our covenant.

At sunset, as Abram slept deeply, God spoke to him in the darkness. He told him about the future hardship and blessing of Abram's offspring.

Then a smoking portable oven and a blazing torch moved between the split animals. Were these fiery objects representations of God? We think of the Exodus when the Lord went ahead of his people in a pillar of fire by night. These burning objects in Abram's vision would be fit figures of God's cleansing zeal, consuming judgment and matchless holiness.

God made a unilateral covenant with Abram and his descendants. Hebrews 6:13 reminds us of another occasion containing the same principle: 'When God made his promise to Abraham, since there was no-one greater for him to swear by, he swore by himself.'

Whether the geographic details of the land were those fulfilled during King David's reign, are guidelines for today's Israel or are still waiting to be realised when the Messiah reigns, the promise of them to Abram gave him hope – not just for himself as an individual but also for posterity. In many cultures the individual realises his or her identity most completely as part of the larger group. Aren't we also the offspring of Abram as we trust in the promise-keeping triune God?

From Ani to Anav

*'So Hagar bore Abram a son, and Abram gave the name Ishmael
to the son she had borne' (v. 15).*

Abram had worried that his servant Eliezer of Damascus would be his heir. God said no. Sarai crafted a plan using another convenient outsider in their household, her Egyptian maid (no doubt acquired on the disastrous visit to Egypt).

Sarai's idea was within legal customary practice of the day. Maybe today a woman who couldn't bear a child would consider finding a surrogate mother. Yet not everything that is legal is within God's best plan. Sarai's desire for a son super- seded other concerns, clouded her judgment and led to unforeseen consequences.

Sarai suggested that her husband have a child with Hagar on his wife's behalf. Abram didn't protest, but took Hagar as a wife. Hagar's ready conception lent her an air of superiority over her barren mistress. Sarai was angry, resented the maid and blamed Abram. Rather than handle the household tension or turn arbiter, Abram let his offended wife deal with the issue.

Not surprisingly, Sarai mistreated Hagar and Hagar fled toward Egypt. The word mistreat, *anah*, is the same word used in Genesis 15:13 as well as in Exodus to describe Egyptian oppression of the Israelites. It can also mean to humble oneself (as in penitence). Another form of the word, *ani*, describes one's suffering, affliction or poverty brought by circumstances imposed by someone else.

A companion word, *anav*, denotes the humble character of one dependent on God. The difference is that the *ani* is needy and *must* depend on God whereas the *anav* chooses to depend on God. It's the attitude Jesus promoted in the beatitudes (Matthew 5). Sometimes God uses suffering to lead us to humility, meekness and trust. To a degree, this was Hagar's experience.

Hagar was unprepared for overwhelming divine concern when she encount- ered the angel of the Lord's mercy for herself and her unborn child. She acknow- ledged the Lord as 'the God who sees me', returned to serve Sarai and deliver Abram's son Ishmael – 'God hears'. She learned that God saw her plight and heard her cry. He cares for today's marginalised people and asks us to as well.

Four New Names

*'But my covenant I will establish with Isaac, whom Sarah will bear
to you by this time next year' (v. 21).*

Hagar, Abram and Sarai learned from the mistakes of managing their situations autonomously. Hagar returned to the household in an attitude of submission or at least cooperation. With some grace or humility, Sarai received her home-made rival back to the tent. Abram learned to submit to God's known will rather than the 'better ideas' of others. They each recognised God's personal concern for and interest in them.

The baby boy was thirteen when God next visited ninety-nine-year-old Abram with fresh promises and a covenant. God identified himself for the first time in Scripture as *El Shaddai* (God the Almighty or Abundant One). This name spoke of great provision. God asked Abram to determine to walk blamelessly in his way. When Abram responded with a humble posture, God gave Abram a new name to signify his promises. Now he was Abraham.

The prospect of producing many descendants including royal lineage, possessing the whole land of Canaan and of covenanting to circumcise all males of the race forever must have been daunting. Wife Sarai would be Sarah and God would bless her with Abraham's own son as the first of copious descendants.

No wonder Abraham fell on his face and laughed, delighted yet incredulous at the idea that a baby could be born to a post-menopausal woman in her nineties. He already had a teenage son; couldn't he be a child of promise? Once again Abraham was seeing things from a natural viewpoint. God assured Abraham that Ishmael would have significance too, but would not be the son of the covenant.

Sarah would bear a son for Abraham and his name would be Isaac ('laughter'). *He* would be the son of the covenant. No wonder God had identified himself as the Almighty, Abundant One. It would take a miracle to bring this promise to pass.

Abraham may have harboured secret doubts about what he had heard, but he exercised obedience and trust in God by taking the next step. He circumcised all males in his household that very day.

Do we know the joy of obeying God's word to us without delay?

Holy Visitor

'Is anything too hard for the Lord?' (v. 14).

His tent pitched in shade of towering trees,
aged Abraham sits seeking breeze
in the heat of the day.
Looks up, curious to see three men nearby,
hurries to meet them, greet them
in the heat of the day.
Invites them stop and be his guests,
to wash their feet with his drawn water,
to rest in shade
while he arranges their midday meal
in the heat of the day.
Agreed, he tells his wife to quickly bake much bread,
runs, chooses calf to slaughter, orders it cooked
in the heat of the day.
Old master serves the meat and milk himself
then stands in waiting under trees
in the heat of the day.
'Where is wife Sarah?' they ask.
'In the tent.'
'She will have a son when I return next year,'
says the Lord
in the heat of the day.
Old Sarah hears, thinks it impossible, distrusts
and stifles a laugh behind floured hands.
'Why did she laugh in disbelief?'
She lies, 'I did not laugh.'
He who knows better, knows all, corrects, 'You did laugh.'
Well, didn't her man laugh out loud for joy at this news
on *El Shaddai's* name-changing visit?
'Is anything too hard for God?'
says the Lord,
in the heat of our day.

E. M.

To ponder:

How do you respond when the Holy Visitor speaks to your heart?

For the Sake of Ten

'Will not the Judge of all the earth do right?' (v. 25).

The visitors have enjoyed bread and butter, meat and milk, and delivered amazing news. The host sees them on their way to Sodom. Abraham would have been in high spirits as he thought of little else than his promised son.

Might they visit his nephew, Lot, with good news too? One of the guests, thought by many to have been an Old Testament appearance of Christ (a theophany), reveals their mission to the soon-to-be-patriarch. The other guests travel ahead while the Lord confides in Abraham.

The mood becomes sombre. Outcries from twin cities Sodom and Gomorrah have reached heaven. Were the outcries from the victims of evil? The Lord expresses his concern and commitment to corrective action.

Abraham knows and trusts God and approaches him on behalf of others (v. 23). He appeals to God's justice. He's concerned about the good people who will be swept away with the evil in judgment. Abraham had personally rescued people from Sodom in battle. Now he intercedes for them as boldly as he'd fought for them. He is concerned for justice for the righteous, even if that means temporarily preserving the wicked.

Abraham was a compassionate intercessor with a firm faith in God's goodness. Do the cries of victims of the wickedness of our cities wail to God? I knew an elderly Christian who prayed for the safety of the citizens of her city every night. Do we intercede mainly for those we know and love, or do we have a wider concern? Does the newscast detailing human suffering across the world or the wail of a siren in our neighbourhoods prompt us to pray?

'The LORD said, "If I find fifty righteous people in the city of Sodom, I will spare the whole place for their sake"' (v. 26). Yet Abraham asked if he only found forty-five, forty, thirty, twenty and finally ten righteous people, would he spare the city? The Lord agreed. Maybe Abraham thought that Lot's family and neighbours whom their faith affected would come to more than ten.

Does our faith inspire neighbours, shopkeepers, fellow patients, co-workers or those who provide services to seek God?

Hurry Up!

*'Early the next morning Abraham got up and returned to the place
where he had stood before the LORD' (v. 27).*

When two of Abraham's visitors (here called angels) arrive in Sodom in the evening, they find Lot at the city gate – the place of important civil and financial transactions. Perhaps he has gained official status. He offers them water to wash, a meal at his house and a place to stay. They protest, but he persists and even bakes them unleavened bread (suggesting haste).

Before saying goodnight, they hear commotion, a horde of men demanding sex with the visitors. Lot tries to dissuade them. The crowd derides him for being an outsider who presumes to impose his standards on them (v. 9). When the men try to break down the door, the angels rescue Lot and foil the mob (either by blinding them with brightness or bringing a dense darkness over the area).

At dawn the plan shifts to high gear as the angels implore Lot to take his family and flee the coming destruction. He delays. Is he frozen by fear or indecision? Is he thinking of last night's mob or of his prospective sons-in-law who thought he was joking when he told them of the city's destruction? Mercifully, the angels seize the family's hands and practically drag them safely out of Sodom.

When an angel exhorts them to flee to the mountains without stopping or looking back, Lot objects and asks for haven in the small city nearby – one of the five cities attacked in Genesis 14. What deters him? Can't he outrun the impending disaster? Doesn't he grasp the magnitude of the situation? Does he fear what's in the mountains or prefer city life? The angel consents and says he'll spare that city, but urges haste. It's critical. The timing of the mission of judgment hinges on Lot being out of harm's way.

Perhaps Lot finally understands when Sodom is burning and he's lost his wife who was literally petrified. Jesus later referred to Lot's wife to urge us to stay focused on the things of the Lord and his coming (Luke 17).

Abraham returns to the spot where he'd pleaded with the Lord for Lot's life. He knows the cause of the billowing smoke but does not yet know Lot's fate. He knows that God is holy, depravity must be judged and God's grace is the only hope for deliverance. So do we.

God Remembers

Give thanks to the LORD, call on his name;
make known among the nations what he has done.

Sing to him, sing praise to him;
tell of all his wonderful acts.

Glory in his holy name;
let the hearts of those who seek the LORD rejoice.

Look to the LORD and his strength;
seek his face always.

Remember the wonders he has done,
his miracles, and the judgments he pronounced,

O descendants of Abraham his servant,
O sons of Jacob, his chosen ones.

He is the LORD our God;
his judgments are in all the earth.

He remembers his covenant forever,
the word he commanded, for a thousand generations,

The covenant he made with Abraham,
the oath he swore to Isaac.

A Parent's Pain

*'Lot and his two daughters left Zoar and settled in the mountains,
for he was afraid to stay in Zoar' (v. 30).*

After all the fuss about not going there, Lot moved away from his chosen refuge city to a cave in the mountains. Why was he afraid to stay in Zoar? Did he think he would be blamed for the tragic end of the nearby cities of the pentapolis? Did he realise that if the Lord had not destroyed Sodom, its evil would have destroyed him? Did he now fear entanglement? Had he learned that his deliverance was God's answer to Abraham's intercession for him?

His daughters devise a scheme and justify it to their own satisfaction. Since they do not discuss it with their father, they must know he would not approve. They probably lack moral principles and are desperate to preserve the family. They lived in Sodom, known for its rampant homosexual behaviour. Under pressure of crises, families that have eroded can implode.

Lot may not have known of their scheme, but he had played a role in the family's demise. He had moved the family to Sodom where values were relative at best. He had not held a standard of righteousness. He was a passive parent, perhaps letting things happen and hoping for the best. His daughters had planned to marry men who had no spiritual discernment. With their skewed values, Lot's daughters did not find incest with their father shameful. They boldly named their offspring *Moab* and *Ben-Ammi* ('of my father' and 'son of my people').

Attrition of values can happen in any family. Vigilance to subtle signs helps. Do we tolerate profanity, ignore irreverence, accept unexamined cultural norms? Do we even discuss such things? Knowing what to keep and what to discard as we live out relevant biblical standards at home requires attention, intention and grace. Parents who want to maintain Christian principles of morality and justice to prepare their dependants for stable independence need help. The Word and the Holy Spirit stand ready to direct and assist us, if we turn to them.

To ponder:

What does the Church offer to shore up the Christian family's values? Are we supporting the effort? Do we pray for it?

Dread, Distrust, Deception or Valour, Trust, Truth

'He is a prophet, and he will pray for you and you will live' (v. 7).

King Abimelech of Gerar protests his innocence and that of his people when God confronts him about Sarah. He does not mean to do anything unethical, but Abraham's half-truth gives him occasion to sin. God who knows the motives in all hearts warns the king. The king fears sin and its consequences and acts immediately – early the next morning.

God doesn't speak to Abraham first. Should he have to? Why didn't Abraham learn his lesson in Egypt? Although Abraham could be fearless and proactive for some causes, fear overtakes him at other times. Powerful leaders intimidate him. Abraham wrongly assumes there is no fear of God in Gerar (v. 11). Even if it had been true, would others' unbelief have made God impotent? We wonder why Abraham plots again and doesn't fear God more than people.

God commands the king to return Sarah to her husband, 'a prophet' who would subsequently pray for the king's welfare (v. 7). The word prophet (*nabi*) appears for the first time in Scripture and carries here a sense of inspiration or intercession rather than declaration or prediction.

The king rebukes Abraham, gives him animals, servants, money and roving rights in his land, then restores Sarah to him. The relieved patriarch does pray for the king as God promised and God heals the sterility of the king, his wife and concubines. What irony that he and Sarah still do not have God's child of promise!

Yet as Abraham prays for Abimelech, does he pray for himself in some way as well? Does the intercessor confess his deception? When forgiveness flows for the king, does it touch the sojourner as well? Does Abraham's experience in Gerar commend valour, trust and truth to him as a preferable course of action in the future?

Sometimes we want to avoid appearing foolish and are tempted to connive. The timeless advice of Proverbs 3:5, 6 counsels: 'Trust in the LORD with all your heart and lean not on your own understanding; in all your ways acknowledge him, and he will make your paths straight.' May the Lord help us!

Who Would Have Thought?

'And she added, "Who would have said to Abraham that Sarah would nurse children? Yet I have borne him a son in his old age"' (v. 7).

Finally, the promise of Abraham's own heir is fulfilled. There will be several more times in Scripture when God chooses and announces a child's name before his birth, but Abraham's Ishmael (God hears) and Isaac (laughter) are the first. God had promised Abraham and Sarah a son twenty-five years before, but only within months of the fulfilment did he allude to a due date (18:10, 14). Knowing how long the wait would be might have disheartened them.

God is not fortuitously late, yet our timetables and his might not mesh. Then we need to ask him for staying power and wisdom to trust him while we wait. Otherwise we may rationalise the desired good ends and use flawed means by manipulating situations or people as Sarah did earlier with Hagar.

The happy couple name their child Isaac, circumcise him at eight days according to the covenant and acknowledge that he is an amazing gift from God. Sarah's earlier laughter of unbelief becomes laughter of joy and wonder.

How old is Isaac when his father celebrates his weaning? He might be anywhere from two to five years old. It should be a joyous occasion. But not everyone is laughing with Sarah.

Is teenage Ishmael mocking Sarah or her little boy? Is he jealous? Does he think God's strategy of giving a baby to senior citizens ludicrous? Sarah can't take the insult and determines to be rid of him and 'that woman', again without good cause. She manoeuvres to keep Hagar's son from sharing Isaac's inheritance. She has no use for her past trophy. The price of her prior calculating use of sex still vexes her. Sarah has not yet learned to trust God and his promises or to see that he often uses people to bring them about.

Some of God's promises are universal. Yet some are for specific situations and people and not to be applied generally. Some are conditional. If in doubt, we need to seek the Holy Spirit's help for discernment. God's promises are reliable and not retractable. He accomplishes them according to his time and through our obedience, not our schedules or stage-managing.

All's Well

'God was with the boy as he grew up' (v. 20).

Sarah's eviction decree for Hagar and Ishmael worries Abraham. Ishmael is the son in whom he's invested time and care. Besides, the custom of his homeland is that if a son is born to the true wife, the man is still responsible for the continued care of the substitute wife and child. God intervenes to assure the elderly father that he need not follow custom in this matter. Although not the child of promise, Ishmael won't be forgotten or cast aside. He'll have significance. God will see to it.

As he has with other instructions from God, Abraham complies quickly – early the next morning. Perhaps he assembled provisions before turning in the previous night. Is there still food left from Isaac's party? Although it is heavy to carry, Abraham gives them enough water to get them to the next well along the way.

Perhaps Hagar miscalculates the distance or becomes lost. Their water runs out. In the wilderness that can mean death. Her active teenager is the first to feel the effects of dehydration and hunger. Hagar puts him in the only shade she can find and sits a good way off (a bow-shot away) so she doesn't have to see him die.

They both sob. When the angel speaks to Hagar, he says God has heard the boy's cries. Hagar is not the only one concerned about her child. The angel speaks of God's plan for Ishmael and directs Hagar to action. When in despair, don't we find that taking some physical action is beneficial? Hagar is to support him with her hand. As she does, God directs her to a well she hasn't seen, where they can quench their thirst.

Does she also begin to see that she can survive without Abraham's resources? Is she recognising that God's limitless supply and care is available even to her? She was taken from her original home in Egypt, lived as a servant and is now a single parent – a woman – on her own. Is God interested in her?

God is with them as they live in the desert. Ishmael's skill as an archer helps support them. His mother finds a wife for him from her homeland. Ishmael will become the patriarch of a people, as God told Abraham would happen.

El Olam

'Abraham planted a tamarisk tree in Beersheba and worshipped GOD there, praying to the Eternal God. Abraham lived in Philistine country for a long time' (vv. 33, 34, MSG).

Abraham encounters King Abimelech who remembers that God blesses his prophet, but also that this man sometimes deceives. The king insists that Abraham show him and his household the kindness he'd extended to the foreigner. The patriarch agrees.

Since they are speaking as equals, Abraham raises an issue about the king's servants who confiscated his well. The king protests ignorance. Abraham continues to press for resolution. In an arid country, water sources are critical. Abraham wants to ensure present and future access to it, so initiates a pact – perhaps the first covenant between equals recorded in Scripture.

Abraham presents sheep and cattle to the king to seal the treaty. He sets apart seven lambs which would particularly witness that the well was his. The name of the place – Beersheba – means either 'well of seven' or 'well of oath'. The words for oath and seven are similar and are each repeated three times in the passage.

The king is satisfied with the terms and returns home. Abraham is satisfied and symbolically plants an evergreen tree (or a whole grove of them) and calls on the name of God, using a new name, *El Olam* – Eternal or Everlasting God. He stays in that area for a long time. We wonder if he stays long enough to sit beneath the grey-green foliage and furrowed bark of a mature tree or see dense masses of pink flowers on its branch tips.

The tamarisk comes in many varieties. The largest grows to a height of fifteen metres. It thrives in saline soil and its foliage can be encrusted with its own salt secretions which limit the growth of other plants until heavy rain washes the salt away. The striking tree or grove at the well would offer both shade and a reminder of the agreement.

Was his stay the beginning of the fulfilment of another promise? God said he would be a blessing to the people among whom he moved (12:2, 3). It must have been a peaceful time for the family. They may have stayed in the area for ten years or more enjoying the shade of the evergreen and the shelter of the Everlasting God.

Trust Test

'Then God said . . . "Sacrifice him there as a burnt offering on one of the mountains I will tell you about"' (v. 2).

Abraham had trusted God while he waited for his promised heir. Now, after Abraham has the son, God asks him for his trust and obedience in a difficult test of devotion. Will Abraham cling to the gift or the giver? Will he still believe God will keep his word?

Abraham had been tested many times before – all within God's providence. Sometimes his tests came directly from God and sometimes through life's situations common to all. Some claim God honours Abraham with this supreme tailor-made test. He is giving him an opportunity to show all generations the value of steadfast faith in God.

Does the patriarch sense the import of the test? Has he begun to 'start trusting the sender'? The Lord wants Abraham and Sarah to worship him more than they adore their son. Could Abraham sing the words of Ruth Tracy: 'All that once I thought most worthy, All of which I once did boast, In thy light seems poor and passing, 'Tis thyself I covet most'?

Whatever his private questions, Abraham obeys God's direction right away – early the next day. Once Abraham had cut enough wood for the burnt offering, he and Isaac leave with their servants. As they are unaware of the real reason for the father-and-son pilgrimage, it's doubtful if Sarah knows either. Is her curiosity, her motherly intuition, aroused?

On the third day of travel, nearly fifty miles from home, Abraham sees the mountain and strikes off with Isaac for the place (2 Chronicles 3:1 says this same Mount Moriah was the location of Solomon's temple in Jerusalem). They relieve the donkey of its burden. The son carries the wood; the father safeguards the fire and knife. Is it the same knife he'd used on newborn Isaac to keep the covenant of circumcision? He came with everything he needed.

Abraham's steps seem steady and determined. Isaac is the one who raises the obvious question about the lamb. The New Testament tells us that Abraham reasoned that God could raise his son from the dead (Hebrews 11:19). Had the patriarch's life lessons resulted in an eternal perspective? Had he finally dedicated everything to God, whatever the outcome? Have we?

Vital Faith

I want the faith of God,
Great mountains to remove,
Full confidence in Jesus' blood,
The faith that works by love.

The faith that will rejoice,
To saints by Jesus given,
That turns the key of Paradise
And saves from earth to heaven.

I want the faith that wears,
That can Jehovah see,
That glad life's heaviest burden bears,
That grips eternity.

The faith that cannot fail,
That makes salvation sure,
Anchored within the heavenly veil,
The faith that will endure.

I want the faith that fires,
And gives me heat and light,
That all my soul with zeal inspires,
That makes me love to fight.

The faith that saves from sin,
That will for victory strive,
That brings the power of God within
And keeps my soul alive.

William Pearson (*SASB* 733)

In the 1860s William J. Pearson, then a Methodist lay leader, was a mentor to Amos and Annie Shirley of Coventry during their stay in Derby, England. The Shirleys, with daughter Eliza, became pioneer Salvationists to Philadelphia, USA, in the late 1870s. All four became Salvation Army officers. They, like Abraham, knew the challenges and blessings of living by faith in unchartered territory.

Jehovah Jireh

'So Abraham called that place The LORD Will Provide' (v. 14).

Deliberately, Abraham builds an altar, arranges wood on it, binds his son and lays him on top. Isaac must have been puzzled – and not a little fearful! Does he most fear the fire's heat or his father's intentions? Is the father or son more grateful to hear the voice from heaven: 'Do not lay a hand on the boy' (v. 12)? Who cries more incessantly with relief when the ram appears? Who skips down the mountain with the lighter heart? Who remembers *Jehovah Jireh*, the Lord our provider, for the rest of his life?

Jews call this event *Akedah* and use it to represent any martyrdom or willingness to sacrifice. Has the Lord asked you to sacrifice something precious to you? A middle-aged woman was determined to see an unexpected, inconvenient and difficult pregnancy through. When she experienced a miscarriage, she couldn't explain her relief to her friends, but privately said she felt like Abraham – willing to do the hard thing but thrilled when delivered from it.

The sacrifices required of us will differ, and may not be understood by others to involve self-denial. God sometimes wants us to see the measure of our faith in action. How expandable is it? When we obey, he provides.

On your Christian walk, have you experienced God's memorable provision when you've trusted him? Did his Word steady you, give you peace or hope? Did he prompt people to send you just what you needed although they had no idea that what they did was his answer to your prayer? Has the Lord protected you from danger, known or unknown?

We sing with hymnwriter John Newton:

> His call we obey,
> Like Abr'ham of old,
> Not knowing our way,
> But faith makes us bold;
> For though we are strangers,
> We have a good guide,
> And trust, in all dangers,
> The Lord will provide.

Released, Replaced, Rewarded

'Through your offspring all nations on earth will be blessed,
because you have obeyed me' (v. 18).

For hundreds of years artists have portrayed the poignant *Akedah* or binding and sacrifice of Isaac through sculpture and painting. Often they've depicted an angel staying Abraham's upraised right hand from using the knife on Isaac. Some have also shown the lamb.

God asks us to release things we grasp too tightly. When we do, he replaces them with something better and at the same time rewards our obedience. The angel proclaimed a second message on the mountain – one of reward and blessing, a renewal of the promises of Abraham's countless offspring and their role as a conduit of blessing to the whole world.

By the end of chapter 22 we get a hint of what God had set in motion for Abraham's offspring. After returning home, Abraham received word that his brother Nahor and wife had eight sons. One of Nahor's granddaughters would one day be Isaac's wife. Jesus' genealogies in Matthew and Luke include Abraham and Isaac.

What the Old Testament conceals, the New Testament reveals. Abraham's willingness to sacrifice Isaac on Mount Moriah prefaces our Father God's supreme sacrifice in offering Christ the Son on Mount Calvary. Isaac trusted his father who loved him. So did Jesus, who out of love for us willingly paid for our sins with his life.

Abraham's willingness to sacrifice is difficult to understand, but speaks of the power of love that holds nothing back from God. Abraham sacrificed Isaac on his own heart's altar before he laid him on the stone altar. He demonstrated that faith involves risk but there is adventure in continuing to say 'yes' to a God who is wholly trustworthy.

———————

To ponder:

Has God asked you to lay something or someone on the altar? Obedient release brings incomparable reward.

Death of a Princess

'Sarah lived to be a hundred and twenty-seven years old' (v. 1).

New Testament writers share snippets of Sarah's obituary. She is listed in the Hebrews 11 hall of faith. Peter calls her a good example of a godly wife. Paul speaks of Sarah as an illustration of the grace of God. Where could they have said Sarah was from? Ur, Bethel, Beersheba, Hebron? She and Abraham were itinerants, pilgrims. Scripture notes that she died at Kiriath-arba (Hebron) in Canaan. She would not need to move again.

Abraham, her spouse of decades, mourned his cherished partner. His weeping over Sarah is the first time tears of grief are recorded in Scripture. His loss was great. Yet even Sarah's death gave the patriarch opportunity to express faith in God.

Abraham approached the leaders of the land where he lived. He respectfully requested that they sell him a particular cave as a tomb. They offered to sell him the cave along with the field.

He buried his wife in the cave in the field of Machpelah near Mamre (Hebron). With this purchase, Canaan became his homeland. Ironically, this was the only land Abraham owned in the land God promised him. But he was looking to the future and trusting God for this life and the next.

Salvation Army poet and former writer of *Words of Life*, Harry Read, shortly after the loss of his life's partner, wrote:

> My loved one lives! She has but gone before me,
> Her body's weaknesses are left behind.
> She shares the life of Christ in highest glory
> The fullness of her destiny to find.
>
> What then of me? Do I my faith surrender?
> Become a captive bound by memory's chains?
> Can I not live enriched by memory's splendour
> And prove in life and death that Jesus reigns?
>
> Lift up this sometime downcast heart of mine,
> O Lord, and in me too your glory shine.

Forever With the Lord!

'Then Abraham breathed his last and died at a good old age, an old man and full of years; and he was gathered to his people' (v. 8).

A braham and Sarah enjoyed many years together. After Sarah's death, Abraham soon took care of comforting Isaac and seeing to Isaac's future (more about that later). Abraham remarried and had six children. He was generous to all his children, but eventually moved them east – toward where he came from in Mesopotamia and away from Isaac. He arranged for Isaac to inherit everything he owned.

At the time of the covenant described in chapter 15, God had promised Abraham: 'You, however, will go to your fathers in peace and be buried at a good old age' (v. 15). Today's passage shows that several aspects of the promise were fulfilled. Abraham died and was buried at 175, 'a good old age'. The text also says he was 'full of years'. Some translate that phrase 'satisfied with life'.

'In peace' may have connoted the patriarch's being at peace with himself, with his neighbours, with God. We notice that Genesis 25:9 says his sons Isaac and Ishmael buried him in the cave he'd bought when Sarah died. Had the brothers come to some measure of peace between them? Out of respect for their father, had they put any grievances aside to bury him?

One more aspect of 'in peace' may have been that Abraham was buried with Sarah. Only occasionally do loved ones who partner in ministry and journey together go to heaven nearly at the same time. As David sang of King Saul and his son, they were loved in life and not parted in death (2 Samuel 1:23). Sarah had preceded Abraham and 'died in faith' a number of years earlier, yet 'together with the Lord' would have been a fitting inscription at their grave.

Abraham left his material wealth to his offspring and his spiritual wealth to the world. With Abraham's death, God's blessing was transferred to Isaac. Now all who have trusted Christ as Saviour are, like Isaac, children of promise (Galatians 4:28). We are witnesses of salvation by faith in God, walking in obedient faith to the Word. Then we can say with hymnwriter James Montgomery: 'For ever with the Lord! Amen; so let it be!' (*SASB* 877).

Answer To Prayer

*'He will send his angel before you so that you can get a wife
for my son from there' (v. 7).*

Not knowing how many years he has left to live, at 140 Abraham takes care of a huge task – finding a daughter-in-law, a wife for Isaac, a mother for his grandchildren. Although he wants her to be someone from his extended clan in Mesopotamia, he doesn't want Isaac to leave the Promised Land to seek for his bride.

So he entrusts his chief servant, likely Eliezer, with the matrimonial mission. The man has been with Abraham through his journeys, acquisitions, mistakes, victories and covenants. He may have helped his master build altars, dig wells, pitch tents, rout the enemy, entertain heavenly visitors, carry out God's instructions. He watched Isaac develop from infancy to adulthood. Who could be better suited to represent Abraham on this assignment?

Trusting a personal envoy with the task sounds surer than using today's on-line match-making services or marriage brokers. Yet some cultures have perfected the use of go-betweens. Abraham's servant was given few instructions other than where to go to look for a bride for Isaac.

The servant's only hesitation is the response of the woman he will find. Abraham assures the servant that God who has led him for sixty-five years – ever since he called him to leave his homeland – will send his angel to guide him. And if the woman won't come back, the servant is released from responsibility. So they agree with a vow and the mission begins.

Has he ever exercised the faith in God that he's seen in his master? He acts with his master's authority and assurance and uses his master's resources, yet on his own he has many questions. Ten camels, a destination and plenty of presents don't engender enough confidence. He thinks up a plan.

He'll wait at the town's outer limits where the women come for water. He'll ask for a drink. He'll seek one who has the poise to handle unexpected situations. In his anxiety, he prays to the God of his master with a specific selfless request. To his amazement and relief God answers him specifically before he finishes his prayer.

God knows and will answer our heart's specific prayers today.

The Answer Unfolds

'Without saying a word, the man watched her closely to learn whether or not the LORD had made his journey successful' (v. 21).

The servant sees a beautiful young woman, and then quickly discovers her strong inner qualities. She is kind and hospitable to him, a stranger, is willing to do a commonplace job and does it ably. She seems spontaneous and self-motivated. Just one more thing, could she possibly be related to his master's clan? When Rebekah reveals whose daughter and granddaughter she is, everything comes together.

God answers the servant's prayer in every detail and his tenuous faith grows. He dares to bow down in public – like his camels – and worship. Before strangers he praises God for his kindness to Abraham. He testifies: 'The LORD has led me on the journey to the house of my master's relatives' (v. 27).

Some have seen this chapter of Genesis as an illustration of the Father sending his Spirit to find a bride for the Son. The father's love and concern and the servant's selfless search for one who is willing to be the son's bride certainly resembles God's love for the world and his sacrifice to claim each one who in response to his tenderness and forgiveness makes up the Church.

What choices did a woman of that day have? Would she always be just someone's daughter or sister? She'd watered the smelly camels unselfishly. The gifts of jewellery were an unexpected plus. Was she looking for adventure?

Her father and brother both attributed the whole incredible unfolding scenario as 'from the LORD' and consented as one to the servant's request to take Rebekah back with him (v. 50). Was she also convinced of divine guidance? If not, wouldn't her willingness to leave home the next day with the servant of a wealthy and distant relative seem hasty or immature (vv. 56–58)?

She hadn't planned on meeting a match-making servant, but she certainly embraced the opportunity his arrival presented. She believed what he had said and joined the servant's mission by faith. She may have envisioned some of what lay ahead as she left with her family's blessing, but the journey of her life had only begun with her 'I will go' (v. 58). Are we willing to go with God?

He Remembers His Covenant Forever

That day David first committed to Asaph and his associates this psalm of thanks to the LORD:

> Give thanks to the LORD, call on his name;
>   make known among the nations what he has done.
> Sing to him, sing praise to him;
>   tell of all his wonderful acts.
> Glory in his holy name;
>   let the hearts of those who seek the LORD rejoice.
> Look to the LORD and his strength;
>   seek his face always.
> Remember the wonders he has done,
>   his miracles, and the judgments he pronounced,
> O descendants of Israel his servant,
>   O sons of Jacob, his chosen ones.
>
> He is the LORD our God;
>   his judgments are in all the earth.
> He remembers his covenant forever,
>   the word he commanded, for a thousand generations,
> the covenant he made with Abraham,
>   the oath he swore to Isaac.

Adieu and 'I do'

*'He went out to the field one evening to meditate, and as he looked up,
he saw camels approaching' (v. 63).*

Abraham's servant and his companions, Rebekah and her maids and their ten camels struck out for the south. Although they no doubt covered the distance as quickly as possible, it was a long trip with plenty of time for hearing more details of Isaac's family, and for thinking.

What was she expecting of him and he of her? Forty-year-old Isaac was the heir and the only child of Sarah and Abraham. Rebekah had a brother. Isaac's mother had died. Rebekah's parents were living. She did not know the grief of losing a parent. She had lived in a town. He lived in a tent. Would they understand one another?

She first saw her groom in the evening. He was out in the field meditating when he saw the camels, and Rebekah saw him. In propriety she covered her face. After the servant related a full explanation of the expedition to those who'd waited at home, the heir married the girl from Haran and loved her. Their marriage comforted Isaac. They would have thirty-five years of Abraham's oversight, twenty years of it childless.

Isaac was a man of peace who negotiated compromises over conflict – especially related to finding fresh water and tending wells. When God affirmed his covenant with Isaac it was in conjunction with a well (26:19–24). Although his name wasn't changed and there was no dramatic encounter, it was the vital assurance he needed. He responded by building an altar (26:25).

God works through the circumstances of those who trust him. Although out of sight, he was the cause of all that happened in this story. In this longest chapter of Genesis there is no overt miracle, prophecy or covenant. The servant prayed, then looked for evidences of God at work and found them.

At many points, things could have gone awry. But in God's providence, as the servant was faithful to his specific mission, God saw to his greater plan. The servant and the son were blessed and had more cause to praise God than they realised. Those who do the will of God are used by God, albeit often unawares.

Sturdy Shoes for the Long Trek
(Letter of Jude)

Introduction

We turn to a brief book not recently commented on in *Words of Life*. Since it contains only 25 verses, consider reading it in several different translations.

We notice many similarities between Jude and 2 Peter. Why is this? Were both authors riveted on rooting out false itinerant teachers? Does Peter borrow from Jude, or Jude from Peter? Or did both have the same core source and just happen to write at the same time? No one is certain.

Jude probably wrote his letter in the latter half of the first century, possibly around the same time James, his brother, wrote his Epistle. The book may have been written in Palestine or Egypt.

Like James, Jude wrote a general letter to dispersed Jewish converts. Like James, Jude used Old Testament references and assumed his readers were acquainted with Jewish literature. Was a rich foundation and appreciation for reading or learning fostered in their childhood home where Jesus also grew up?

Stylistically, Jude frequently set his illustrations, descriptions and references in threes.

Jude addressed crucial issues passionately. We can almost hear him reciting some of the psalms that plead with God to overthrow those who have attacked his people and sullied his name. He deplored false teaching. Yet he advised a considerate approach toward those who, affected by it, had sinned. And he knew that those who know God's mercy themselves are best able to extend it.

When he urged believers to stand firm he didn't mean they should stand still. He intended steadfastness and action as if he advocated sturdy shoes with good tread for a long, rough trek.

Kept Blameless

'Mercy, peace and love be yours in abundance' (v. 2).

Since Jude is just one chapter long, it could easily be overlooked. Perhaps the most familiar verses of its twenty-five are the final two which are used as a benediction. Yet the entire short Epistle written as a circular letter has continued significance. The books of Jude, James, 1 and 2 Peter and 1, 2 and 3 John share the category of general letters not written to specific people or particular churches or locations.

Verse 2 shows Jude's attitude of love and concern toward his readers. His letter demonstrates practical care by warning believers about those who mean to destroy the Church through heresies. We all need God's mercy, peace and love, but especially so when we live among subtle evil which erodes or challenges our faith.

Who is Jude? He tells us he is a servant of Jesus Christ and a brother of James (v. 1). Although there have been several theories, it is widely thought that the James he refers to is the half-brother of Jesus, author of the Epistle of James and leader of the early Christian Church. Jude's modest introduction of himself only as Jesus' servant and James' brother carries a stamp of humility. Those who would know who James was should catch the note of authority Jude's letter carries.

Like his brother James, Jude refers to Jesus as Lord. Jesus' brothers did not recognise him as Messiah until after his resurrection, so it is a testimony of their faith in Christ's divinity to purposely and repeatedly call him Lord. From his own earlier experience, Jude may have understood the perspective of people whose theories denied Christ's Lordship.

In verse 1, Jude addresses his letter to those who have been called or summoned (past), are loved by God (present) and kept by Christ (ongoing toward the future). Or as one version declares: 'kept for Jesus Christ' (*ASV*). It implies that those who continue to trust Christ are being preserved until his coming. God's call, love and keeping undergird believers when doubt and dissent swirl around us. The apostle Paul also prayed: 'May your whole spirit, soul and body be kept blameless at the coming of our Lord Jesus Christ' (1 Thessalonians 5:23).

Vying for the Faith

'They are godless men, who change the grace of our God into a licence for immorality and deny Jesus Christ our only Sovereign and Lord' (v. 4).

Jude says he'd intended to write about the salvation he and his readers held in common, but finds he must instead rally them to contest for the faith. That faith was Christianity. Its basics, committed to believers once for all, were to be maintained and defended through firm doctrine and moral living (v. 3). The Holy Spirit guides the application of its principles.

People with skewed doctrine had infiltrated the Church to spread their ideas. These were not confused believers, but intruders who came to spread their 'better', more sophisticated philosophies. They perverted the gospel by teaching that grace gives physical licence and that Jesus is not Lord. They lived immorally and taught heretically. Jude doesn't lay out an argument as a theologian or lawyer, but does denounce their apostasies.

This ever-recurring antinomianism (changing the grace of God into licence for blatant immorality) materialises in various guises within the Church. In his *Daily Study Bible Series*, William Barclay reminds us that 'Jude's heretics have existed in every Christian generation'. George Fox and Richard Baxter encountered and refuted those who perverted grace for their own gratification. John Wesley and John Bunyan did as well.

The other major heresy Jude likely countered was Gnosticism. He refers to it when he says that some deny Jesus Christ, our only Sovereign Lord (v. 4). If they were Gnostics, they denied the oneness of God, the humanity and uniqueness of Jesus and set up intellectual distinctions and divisions in the Church.

We may wonder how sensible people could be swept up with such thinking. No doubt it happened gradually and subtly. Should it make us pause today? If the heresies had been self-evident to the Church of his day, Jude wouldn't have been compelled to point out deceptive apostates who distort grace, deny Christ's Lordship and deserve condemnation.

Although pressing issues restrained Jude from writing the affirming letter he'd hoped to write, at the finale he will yet address salvation in Christ and the joy, hope and victory it produces.

Take Care!

*'Though you already know all this, I want to remind you that the
Lord delivered his people out of Egypt, but later destroyed those
who did not believe' (v. 5).*

In one of his many sets of triplets, Jude gives historic examples from the Old
Testament and Jewish tradition to illustrate the doom of those who don't
continue in the faith. The initial readers would have been acquainted with his
references.

The people who were corrupting the Church didn't think of themselves as anti-
Christian, but as a more advanced, superior class. To show that people of privilege
can go astray, Jude reminds them of the Israelites whom God delivered from
Egypt. Subsequently those who abandoned their faith in God were sentenced to
wander in the wilderness until they died. If that could happen to the Israelites, it
could happen to anyone who thought themselves privileged – even ungodly
people within 'new Israel' or the Church.

Once again Jude refers to a privileged group that went astray and suffered
judgment. He writes of the angels. He may have chosen to mention angels because
of the Jews' elaborate belief in angels or to counter the heretics' apparent stance
against angels (v. 8).

Jude's third example is Sodom and Gomorrah whose destruction by fire as a
type of God's wrath against sin was legendary. Were the false teachers trying to
lead some of Jude's readers into the type of immorality known in Sodom? Do
Jude's references to Sodom tie to Lot's angelic visitors and what the men of the city
intended to do to them?

It is as if Jude jogs our memory about what happens when people flagrantly
disregard God, his moral laws and warnings. Then he warns that their fiery
punishment is only a shadow of the fate of those who deny God's truth, so repent
now!

Unbelieving Israelites died in the wilderness, unfaithful angels are bound in
darkness, Sodom and Gomorrah were burned up. As Paul reminds us in another
Epistle, 'So, if you think you are standing firm, be careful that you don't fall! . . .
But when you are tempted, he will also provide a way out so that you can stand up
under it' (1 Corinthians 10:12, 13).

Wide of the Mark

'Woe to them! They have taken the way of Cain; they have rushed for profit into Balaam's error; they have been destroyed in Korah's rebellion' (v. 11).

Jude asserts that the dreamers (corrupters of the faith) defile their bodies like the people of Sodom, and despise authority like Israelites in the wilderness who rejected the authority of both Moses and God and defame celestial beings. They mistakenly think their immorality, insubordination and irreverence can fulfil their lives.

From the apocryphal story (familiar to his readers) of Michael contending for the body of Moses, Jude makes his point about not speaking against angels. If Michael wouldn't speak against a fallen angel but left it to the Lord to rebuke him, surely no person should speak against the heavenly angels. Whatever the false prophets were saying against the angels, their attitude was sufficiently off the mark for Jude to have to deal with it.

To underscore the false teachers' state, Jude compares them with Cain, Balaam and Korah, who ran after the wrong things and perished in sin. Perhaps Jude chose these three particular figures to also hint at the Gnostic heresy that these villains were heroes.

Cain was the world's first murderer. In Hebrew tradition he also represents anyone who doesn't believe in God or morality, so justifies doing whatever he pleases. Balaam's incidents reveal a man who chose to sin for gain (Numbers 22–24) and who taught others to sin as well (Numbers 31). Jude's third example was Korah (Numbers 16). He revolted against God's appointed leaders and thereby against God. In his pride he grasped for things he shouldn't have and suffered radical consequences.

We wonder at the immaturity of the false teachers. They were ready to mock what they didn't understand and allow brute appetites to rule their judgment. They were keen to gratify their senses, yet blind and deaf regarding things of God and truth.

Jude shakes us out of indifference to things that can pollute and dilute our faith in Christ. May God help us to be conscious of what lies behind some 'politically correct' views in our culture and to seek, teach and live reliable, biblically based doctrine for our sakes and that of others.

Disquieting Mural

'Know that the LORD is God. It is he who made us, and we are his;
we are his people, the sheep of his pasture' (Psalm 100:3).

Jude further describes the fully-fledged sensualists through an array of metaphors. Step into his gallery. See a huge mural full of bold colours and strong images that depict emptiness and futility. Think of the verses as a landscape painting in several satirical sections.

One shows early Christians at a shared meal (love feast). At first glance there is fellowship. But muddy blotches splatter the spread. Sheep gather around shepherds hopeful of being led to green pastures, but the shepherds are irritated with any interruption of their own indulgence and carousing. (We think of Ezekiel 34, a whole chapter of God's indictment of such unsuitable shepherds.)

A parched field is overshadowed by clouds. Rain barrels are ready. The leaves stir, but the clouds blow past. There is no rain. An autumn orchard produces no fruit. Empty baskets are strewn about. Some trees are uprooted as if by a storm.

Gale-driven waves toss oil-covered flotsam and jetsam. The waves retreat, but the debris and dirty spume remain on shore. Overhead, shooting stars fizzle out as quickly as fireworks in the night sky. Spent, they become part of eternal chaotic darkness.

This is no global-warming dystopia. The surreal scene depicts the state of the hearts and influence of false prophets.

The apostates are the blotches ruining the fellowship of the Church; the selfish shepherds who show no care for others; the empty clouds, the fruitless uprooted trees which seem full of promise, but are useless; the murky waves bent on polluting; the burned-out stars headed for the abyss. From the book of Enoch which Jewish readers would recognise, Jude indicates that the Lord's coming will bring deserved judgment.

An audio track accompanying the painting would reverberate with discordant murmurs of grumbling, fault-finding, boasting and flattering. Are their offspring still here?

May God help us to discern spiritual truth from treachery and to live openly before him who made us, redeemed us and keeps us through Christ our Lord!

New Step

I hear the sound of shuffling feet
along life's rugged road.
They tell of one who walks alone
beneath a heavy load.
The toil of life, the stress and care
beat on like muffled drums,
Their cadence marks the steps he takes
as down the road he comes.

I've heard the sound of shuffling feet
along his path before.
It is the walk of all oppressed,
the weak, the sick, the poor.
Not in the things as judged by men
does God their footsteps see.
It is the weight upon the heart
that makes them less than free.

God sees the step and knows the heart
and longs to set men free.
The weak in heart, the sick in soul,
the poor are you and me.
There is a friend who walks beside
and every burden shares;
The rugged road will seem more smooth
just knowing Jesus cares.

Larry Bosh

Forewarned, Forearmed

'But you, dear friends, build yourselves up in your most holy faith and pray in the Holy Spirit' (v. 20).

The word in verse 12 which some have translated 'spots', 'blotches' or 'blemishes' can also mean hidden treacherous reefs. If so, then Jude warns believers that their Christian fellowship is like a ship heading for unseen submerged danger when they listen to the apostates with inflated egos.

He wants them to beware of the agitators' duplicity as they pander to any with power or influence. Further, their sensuality is evidence of their general lack of self control. Identify and watch out for the errors of these false teachers and steer clear of their false doctrine that could shipwreck your faith, he says.

Jude reminds readers of what the apostles repeatedly said about expecting such scoffers and self-gratifiers to show up in the end times (v. 18). Paul warned Ephesians of savage wolves that would seek to destroy the flock (Acts 20:29–31) with distortions of truth. Peter spoke to the same issue (2 Peter 2:1–3).

Jude says that apostates seek to divide the Church and are not spiritually minded or guided by the Holy Spirit. In sharp contrast, true believers should keep growing, stay grounded in sound biblical faith and pray from hearts empowered by the Holy Spirit.

In his *The Cost of Discipleship* Dietrich Bonhoeffer warned Christians against 'cheap grace' devoid of the demands of the cross and the living Christ. He said, 'Our struggle today is for costly grace.' Seek what Jesus wants of us rather than what the fads or fashions of momentarily popular tangents of faith lure us to embrace.

Our desire may be summed up in a Salvation Army chorus:

> To be like Jesus!
> This hope possesses me,
> In every thought and deed,
> This is my aim, my creed;
> To be like Jesus!
> This hope possesses me,
> His Spirit helping me,
> Like him I'll be.
>
> *John Gowans*

League of Mercy

*'Keep yourselves in God's love as you wait for the mercy of our
Lord Jesus Christ to bring you to eternal life' (v. 21).*

In verse 20 Jude speaks of praying in the Spirit. We certainly need the Holy Spirit's discernment to distinguish which approach to take with those Jude advises action toward. As the Spirit prompts our hearts and guides our prayers we will be able to know how best to show mercy.

Jude instructs the Church to show mercy to those who doubt and waver. Meanwhile, snatch some up from sin as if rescuing them from fire. And show a strong mercy born of fear and repulsion as if of the life-threatening infection on the stained spiritual clothes of others.

We protest that we are neither inoculated against deadly diseases nor trained for emergency rescues, to use Jude's metaphors. But can't we all show mercy in some way toward those who are flirting with error or embroiled in sin? Isn't it still the Church's mission to reclaim the lost?

The expert in law who asked Jesus about requirements for eternal life knew that he should love God and his neighbour, but thought he'd rationalise it by asking just who he should consider his neighbour to be. Jesus replied with the parable of the Good Samaritan and the concluding question: who was a neighbour to the man in distress? The legal expert carefully avoided saying 'the Samaritan' but had to admit, ' "The one who had mercy on him." Jesus told him, "Go and do likewise" ' (Luke 10:37).

We want to be fortified in our faith while not retreating to a merely defensive position, but prepared to engage in the gospel's rescue work as Jesus did. God will help to keep us balanced if we ask him.

Only those who are grounded in the faith and know God's great mercy can engage the lost. We ourselves are looking for the coming of Christ. So we purpose to keep the faith without self-righteousness and stay centred in God's love, waiting with expectation for his great mercy in bringing us into eternal life.

———————

To ponder:

'Blessed are the merciful, for they will be shown mercy'
(*Matthew 5:7*)

Grand Finale

*'To the only God, our Saviour through Jesus Christ our Lord,
be glory, majesty, dominion, and authority, before all time
and now and forever. Amen' (v. 25, RSV).*

Jude ends where he had wanted to begin when he opened his letter to those called, beloved and kept by God. He had intended to write an upbeat paper on the faith, but unexpected trouble in the Church compelled him to write disapprovingly of the distorted doctrine of ungodly people and to encourage believers to stay steadfast in Christ.

In his final verses he writes a doxology that joyfully, hopefully, confidently commends his readers to God who alone is worthy of worship.

One translation starts verse 24 with 'but' and shows more plainly that these final words in Jude are meant to stand in juxtaposition to the earlier warnings. In contrast with the perils Jude exposed and the warnings he issued, the end of the letter stands out as pure promise and praise. It's a bright full moon against a dark night sky.

Face trials and heresies, stand firm in your faith but look up! See the bigger final picture and rejoice!

See Jude's encouragement:

God is able. Hallelujah!

He is able to keep us. In 2 Timothy 1:12 Paul writes in the same vein: 'I know whom I have believed, and am convinced that he is able to guard what I have entrusted to him for that day.'

He is able to keep us from falling. Does he make us more surefooted, smooth the path ahead or rope us to him so that if we start to fall, he helps bear our weight?

He is able to present us blameless in the presence of his glory. What a promise for each Christian who continues to trust the Saviour for salvation!

He is able to present us like sure-footed gazelles, leaping for joy – not necessarily the way we would think to approach God. But by his grace, we are presented to God with joy – both Jesus' and ours.

Jude attaches 'Saviour' to God. Other New Testament writers do so as well at times. Here Jude honours God who is our Saviour through Jesus Christ our Lord: *To him be glory, majesty, dominion, power!*

On a Mission

Introduction

We visit ten chapters of Matthew not commented on in *Words of Life* in recent years. First we look at Matthew 19, 20, 22, 24, 25 and 26. After the Advent segment, we finish the year with a backward glance at the first four chapters of Matthew.

In August, when we paused from our Matthew readings at the end of chapter 18, Jesus was still in Galilee. Now, as we start up with chapter 19, Jesus has left Galilee. On the way to Jerusalem he ministers as he goes through a region east of the Jordan River. As usual, he is followed by crowds who need his healing. During Holy Week he spends time on the Mount of Olives speaking of the future, and in chapter 25 he teaches some characteristics of those looking for his kingdom – readiness, involvement and compassion. To relate to his hearers he grounds his parables in familiar situations from weddings to business. We end the segment with Jesus anointed in Bethany.

At the year end, we will look back to the beginning of Matthew.

In Love, not Legalism

*'So they are no longer two, but one. Therefore what God has
joined together, let man not separate'* (v. 6).

Jesus ended his Galilean ministry and moved into an area of Judea east of the Jordan River where he ministered to the crowds that followed him as usual. There, too, sceptical leaders sought him out with their difficult religious questions. Matthew says their motivation was to test Jesus. They came with the divisive and complicated issue of divorce.

There were two schools of Jewish thought on this at the time. One held the door wide open to divorce for nearly any reason, treating marriage lightly and women as objects. The other narrowed the way to divorce to instances of infidelity. The Pharisees were asking Jesus which view he favoured. Jesus didn't side with either school.

He reminded them of the purpose of marriage by referring to God joining the original couple in an indivisible bond. Since God joins a man and woman, marriage should be seen as a high calling and a lasting relationship on multiple levels.

The Hebrew word for marriage is similar to one for a consecrated offering which is set apart for God and shouldn't be taken back. But this ideal isn't easy and some wanted a way out. The Pharisees persisted.

Why did Moses command a man to give a certificate of divorce and dismiss his wife? Jesus replied that Moses permitted (not commanded) divorce because of men's hard hearts. Did Jesus imply that since men easily divorced women they did not value women and acted out of convenience? Jesus' ministry elevated women in a way that the culture didn't understand. If his teaching about the permanence of marriage astonished the disciples, imagine what the Pharisees thought!

Jesus reminded his hearers that the principle of divorce wasn't a law but a concession to be used when the ideal that God had planned was not upheld. As Jesus exhibited, love not legalism should be the approach in such situations. We wonder if he might have been thinking of the righteous yet kind way Joseph had planned to deal with Mary before the angel told him that her conception of Christ was uniquely of the Holy Spirit.

Every Child

'Jesus said, "Let the little children come to me, and do not hinder them, for the kingdom of heaven belongs to such as these"' (v. 14).

It seems natural for Matthew to include an incident about children after writing about marriage. In Jesus' eyes, marriage is esteemed and so are children. This correlates with what Jesus said about children in the previous chapter. When the disciples asked who would be greatest, Jesus called a child and referred to the importance of having such childlike characteristics as humility, dependence and trust in God. He said that welcoming a child in his name was the same as welcoming him.

In this incident parents, probably mothers, do something customary when they bring young children to a rabbi for a blessing. Are the disciples protective of Jesus, or tired, stressed or accustomed to shooing away children? Do they think toddlers will distract from Jesus' ministry?

Don't the disciples remember what Jesus said earlier about welcoming children? Jesus intervenes. Let the children come. The kingdom of heaven is made up of such as these. To such as these the kingdom belongs.

What Jesus says isn't licence for children to rule or to selfishly disrupt others' opportunity for worship. He advises welcoming them with loving kindness and an attitude of blessing and expectancy. Children learn what they live. Unlocking the possibilities within each child takes careful, intentional nurturing.

In *From the Ground Up*[1] Kathryn Copsey, Project Leader of CURBS (Children in Urban Situations), outlines insights into the spiritual world of the child gained through working with urban children. She explores the biblical perspectives on children which revolve around the 'upside-down' values Jesus demonstrated.

Where do you stand in today's biblical scene? Is Jesus' hand on your head? Do you facilitate others' blessing? Do you need to be reminded that all are welcome? What does Jesus say to us as parents, children, disciples?

Win–win

'Jesus answered, "If you want to be perfect, go, sell your possessions
and give to the poor, and you will have treasure in heaven.
Then come, follow me"' (v. 21).

Although Matthew, Mark and Luke record this incident, only Luke says the inquirer was a ruler and only Matthew says he was young. All label him rich.

The young man says he is seeking eternal life. Although used more by John than others, this is the first time the phrase is used in the Gospels. Eternal life could mean the life to come. One commentator says it means a full and permanent fellowship with God. Another says that here eternal life means a godly life.

The seeker asks what good thing he should do to accomplish his goal. No doubt he was used to achieving whatever he set out to do. Jesus answers him in the same vein. What should you do? Keep the commandments. The man counters, which ones? Jesus enumerates those that deal with how people treat and think of others. The man claims to have done so, but knows something is still missing. Perhaps he had kept the letter of the law, but not the spirit of it.

When Jesus challenges him to know wholeness by selling his possessions, giving to the poor and then following him, it's too much of a sacrifice. Unlike Zaccheus, whose heart was so changed when he met Christ that he voluntarily gave away half of his goods plus repaid with interest anyone he'd cheated, this unnamed rich man clutches his possessions and misses gaining the best of all. Money was his goal, not God.

Comments William Barclay: 'If a man looks on his possessions as given to him for nothing but his own comfort and convenience, they are a chain which must be broken; if he looks on his possessions as a means to helping others, they are his crown.'[2]

We may not have riches, but we're challenged to surrender whatever we cherish more than God and give him first place. It's a win–win offer.

Grace of Giving

The people rejoiced at the willing response of their leaders, for they had given freely and wholeheartedly to the LORD. David the king also rejoiced greatly. David praised the LORD in the presence of the whole assembly, saying,

'Praise be to you, O LORD,
   God of our father Israel,
   from everlasting to everlasting.
Yours, O LORD, is the greatness and the power
   and the glory and the majesty and the splendour,
   for everything in heaven and earth is yours.
   Yours, O LORD, is the kingdom;
   you are exalted as head over all.
Wealth and honour come from you;
   you are the ruler of all things.
   In your hands are strength and power
   to exalt and give strength to all.
Now, our God, we give you thanks,
   and praise your glorious name.

'But who am I, and who are my people, that we should be able to give as generously as this? Everything comes from you, and we have given you only what comes from your hand. We are aliens and strangers in your sight, as were all our forefathers. Our days on earth are like a shadow, without hope. O LORD our God, as for all this abundance that we have provided for building you a temple for your Holy Name, it comes from your hand, and all of it belongs to you. I know, my God, that you test the heart and are pleased with integrity. All these things have I given willingly and with honest intent. And now I have seen with joy how willingly your people who are here have given to you. O LORD, God of our fathers Abraham, Isaac and Israel, keep this desire in the hearts of your people forever, and keep their hearts loyal to you.'

Valuable Need

'Yes, I repeat, a camel could more easily squeeze through the eye of a needle than a rich man get into the kingdom of God!' (v. 24, JBP).

The man who overvalued riches shuffles away disappointed. Then Jesus uses the sad encounter to teach the disciples a life lesson. He starts with an illustration that's bigger than life to make his point. How difficult is it for a rich man to enter the kingdom of heaven? 'It's easier to gallop a camel through a needle's eye' (v. 24, *MSG*).

A Jewish proverb in the Talmud said that even in your dreams you don't see an elephant pass through the eye of a needle. It came from the Babylonian Talmud where the elephant was known. In Palestine the camel was the large animal equivalent. It was a common Jewish expression for anything that was rare or difficult.

The disciples are dumbfounded. For one thing, Jewish tradition held that riches were evidence of God's blessing. So it followed that if a rich person couldn't easily enter the kingdom, probably no one could.

Jesus was challenging their assumptions. He paused before he replied. His look must have etched what he said into the disciples' minds. 'Jesus looked at them intently and said, "For humans this is impossible, but for God all things are possible"' (v. 26, *ISV*).

It's true that riches can foster a false sense of security, tend to tie people to things and hinder generosity, but it doesn't have to be so. There are enough biblical, historical and current-day examples of wealthy people of faith to show that. But anything that lessens our sense of dependence on God can begin the dangerous tendency toward replacing him.

Peter blurts out a question. What could they expect as reward for leaving everything for Jesus' sake? The Master gives a parable in mild rebuke, but first affirms his followers' self-denial. They can expect to share Christ's triumph in heaven. On earth they will gain more relationships and things than they sacrifice. They will know eternal life. They will participate in the great surprises and reversals of God's judgment in the end. What expectations!

To ponder:

What is the value of our need in propelling us to God?

A Day's Wage for a Day's Work?

'So the last will be first, and the first will be last' (v. 16).

The discussion set off by the rich man's questions and that of Peter continues. Through a story, Jesus rebukes Peter's attitude of expecting or seeking reward.

Jesus' parable is about day labourers. In the USA, day labour is a nationwide, year-round reality. Tens of thousands work as day labourers. Most are male and are immigrants from Mexico or Central America. They mainly do odd jobs for homeowners or work in the construction and gardening sectors. They rely on their day-to-day wages as their sole income. Most live on the threshold of poverty.

The people hired in the parable may have had similar situations. Jesus says the kingdom of heaven is like a landowner who hires workers for his vineyard from sun-up to sundown (actually at 6 a.m., 9 a.m., noon, 3 p.m. and 5 p.m.). He promises to pay them at the going rate for a day labourer or a Roman soldier.

There's nothing unusual about the situation thus far. But when the day is done the owner wants his manager to pay out wages starting with those who began work just an hour earlier and going in reverse. The first to be paid must have been surprised and delighted to receive a full day's pay, even though they were hired near the day's end. Just as surprised, but not delighted, were those who had worked all day but also received a day's pay and no more. Their complaint was that the landowner had treated the workers as equal in spite of a very different workload.

If privileged to enter the kingdom early in church history or in our own lives, early arrival is not an entitlement but an opportunity. Have we entered the kingdom further along in its history or in our own years? We are just as cherished by God. Status of service is the same with God. It's not the amount given, but the love and spirit in which it is given and whether it represents our best response to his great love. Such is his grace.

Concerning Peter's question of reward, and its inference of deserving to be ranked first, Jesus reminds him and us: first now is last later; last now is first later.

Selflessly Yours

'Not so with you. Instead, whoever wants to become great among
you must be your servant' (v. 26).

For the third time Jesus tells the disciples privately of his coming death (vv. 17–19). Matthew, Mark and Luke include all three of these disclosures. Do the disciples comprehend what Jesus reveals? He does not hide the cross or his suffering from them. But he ends on a note of hope and victory when he speaks boldly of his resurrection.

Shortly after his reference to his Passion in chapter 17, they insensitively ask who will be the greatest in the kingdom. He illustrates the value of humility through a child he places in their circle.

After his heart-rending revelation this time there's another misplaced question. Zebedee's wife and her disciple sons, James and John, approach Jesus for assurance of positions in the kingdom. Their mother might have overheard Jesus telling the disciples they would sit on thrones in heaven. They come with the posture of worship, but the request is for position.

Jesus *only* asks if they can go through what he will go through. They answer yes without a second thought. Besides being ambitious, are they overconfident or naïve? They at least exhibit faith that there actually will be a kingdom in which Jesus will reign.

The other ten disciples are indignant with James and John. Jesus is patient with them all. He knows they still don't grasp his message. He offers another paradox for them to ponder. It contradicts the spirit of the world: serving precedes greatness, sacrifice precedes success. He reminds them that he, their Master, came to serve and to give his life to ransom others.

The Christian life does involve a 'cup' although it comes in varied forms. Some experience martyrdom, many more have opportunity to faithfully live a daily sacrifice through the long haul of suffering in its countless configurations. A mindset of serving Christ humbly and cheerfully in whatever life brings honours the Lord.

There will be rewards – now (here) *or* then (there). My choice exhibits my heart's desire. The Holy Spirit will help me if I ask him.

Hear, Believe, Ask, Receive

'Ask and it will be given to you; seek and you will find;
knock and the door will be opened to you' (7:7).

Vision Challenged?

The crowd shuffles along Jericho Road
raising dust clouds and a stir with their:
'Jesus is passing! Jesus is passing!'
Two sit at road's rim with closed eyes
feeling more than dust, hearing more than refrain.
Two stand and cry to the hub of the throng,
'Son of David, mercy, Kyrie Eleison, Lord, have mercy',
In unison: *'Lord, Son of David, have mercy on us!'*
The crowd turns on them as one: *'Stop, hush up!'*
Emboldened, again: *'Lord, Son of David, have mercy on us!'*

Two call him 'Lord' and mean 'Messiah'.
Jesus knows.
He hears and halts,
calls back: *'What do you want from me?'*
They plead: *'Lord, we want to see!'*

As deeply moved at heart for these, although but two,
as he has been for full multitudes before,
Jesus touches their eyes.
They see and follow him.
What will they see where he goes next?
Jerusalem, with its palms and crowds, its cross and resurrection,
and always they'll see Jesus.

———

To ponder:

Are we following Jesus wherever he leads? Let's ask the Holy Spirit to open our eyes to fresh ways of spreading the word about our Saviour and empowering others to do so.

His Provision

'Make every effort to live in peace with all men and to be holy; without holiness no-one will see the Lord' (Hebrews 12:14).

Jesus tells a parable which in part was similar to stories told by rabbis of his day. The rabbis' stories dealt with readiness for the king's feast and with stewards of royal robes. In both cases those who took direction seriously and acted responsibly were rewarded and those who didn't lost out. But when Jesus uses familiar examples to convey the nature of the kingdom of heaven, he gives more than merely fables with a moral; his parables declare eternal truths.

We receive invitations complete with date and time. But it was customary in Jesus' day to issue invitations to special occasions without precise times. The final summons came when everything was ready. Refusing that summons was an insult. In the parable, the places left vacant by refusals were filled by other people not expecting such a call.

The Jews had been invited to the divine banquet, but when God's Son came with the summons to attend, they refused. Thus God instructed his invitation to be extended to Gentiles.

God's invitation is to something joyous. Who would want to refuse joy? The excuses for not accepting an invitation can be as justifiable as attending to business or to other matters requiring our attention. But what about what is missed? The hospitality will be extended to others instead.

In Japan, after a traditional bath at a *ryokan* (rural inn), guests may use a cotton *yukata* (summer kimono) imprinted with the name of the inn. On an evening stroll, therefore, one can deduce who is staying where. In this story, the king sent his messengers to the crossroads to gather the willing to the feast. The door was open to all. But those who came needed to be clothed in what was provided.

Salvation is an open call but must be accepted on God's terms. Could the wedding garment of Matthew foreshadow the radiant linen given to Christ's bride (the Church) and represent the righteousness of the saints in Revelation 19:8? Like holiness, its provision depends on the King, but wearing it depends on the guest. Have we accepted God's gracious provision?

Beyond the Temple

'But he who stands firm to the end will be saved' (v. 13).

A few days after Palm Sunday, as Jesus departs the temple area, probably for the final time, the disciples comment on the temple's glorious architecture. The lengthy temple restoration project is still in process, but the marble and gold glisten. Colossal pillars support the surrounding porch roofs. The centre of Judaism would astound any visitor, especially those from outlying areas. No wonder the disciples point it out.

Rather than revel in the building, Jesus replies that its stones won't be left standing. This troubles them. Perhaps they ponder it as they walk with him up the hill. Jesus and his disciples sit down on the Mount of Olives. They can see the temple.

The disciples ask when the temple's destruction will happen. And their perceptive follow-up question is: 'What will be the sign of your coming and the end of the age?' (v. 3). Mark's Gospel says Peter, James, John and Andrew pose the questions (13:3). Jesus' reply, also recorded by Mark and Luke, is the beginning of what is known as the Olivet discourse.

Jesus starts with their last query. What will be the signs of the end? Jesus gives ten: counterfeit messiahs, wars, famines, pestilences, earthquakes, persecution, a turning from the faith spawning betrayals and hatred, deceitful false prophets, lovelessness and lawlessness and the evangelisation of the world. Do we recognise such trends in current news? When Jesus adds the encouragement of our key verse for the disciples, it's a word for us as well.

Did Jesus see more than the city and the temple that day? The village of Bethany, home of his friends Lazarus, Mary and Martha, lay just to the south. Gethsemane lay in the valley that separated the Mount of Olives from Jerusalem. Calvary was outside the city on another hill.

In her song, 'When Jesus looked o'er Galilee' (*SASB* 103), Catherine Baird wonders if Jesus saw the cross, the crown of thorns, the road to Calvary prefigured in natural settings around him. What was on Jesus' mind on Olivet just days before his Passion for our sakes? Might it have been Catherine Baird's thought of sweeping winds triumphantly declaring 'The Lord shall live again!'?

God's Faithfulness

I will sing of the LORD's great love forever;
  with my mouth I will make your faithfulness known through all
  generations.
I will declare that your love stands firm forever,
  that you established your faithfulness in heaven itself . . .

The heavens praise your wonders, O LORD,
  your faithfulness too, in the assembly of the holy ones.
For who in the skies above can compare with the LORD?
  Who is like the LORD among the heavenly beings?
In the council of the holy ones God is greatly feared;
  he is more awesome than all who surround him.
O LORD God Almighty, who is like you?
  You are mighty, O LORD, and your faithfulness surrounds you . . .

The heavens are yours, and yours also the earth;
  you founded the world and all that is in it.
You created the north and the south;
  Tabor and Hermon sing for joy at your name.
Your arm is endued with power;
  your hand is strong, your right hand exalted.

Righteousness and justice are the foundation of your throne;
  love and faithfulness go before you.
Blessed are those who have learned to acclaim you,
  who walk in the light of your presence, O LORD.
They rejoice in your name all day long;
  they exult in your righteousness.
For you are their glory and strength,
  and by your favour you exalt our horn.
Indeed, our shield belongs to the LORD,
  our king to the Holy One of Israel.

Watching for Him

*'So you also must be ready, because the Son of Man will come
at an hour when you do not expect him' (v. 44).*

To the disciples' question about the destruction of the temple, Jesus gives specific details which many believe were predictions of the Roman siege of Jerusalem in AD 70 when the temple was destroyed by Titus Caesar. The Islamic Dome of the Rock shrine, built in the seventh century, now occupies the temple mount. Only the western wall of the temple platform base remains. Since medieval times that wall has been a well-used place of prayer. Jews pray there daily. Thousands of white prayer papers are tucked into crevices between the stones.

Historian Josephus says that during the first-century siege that razed the temple, more than a million Jews died. Many died of starvation because they gathered in the city where food stores were quickly depleted. Perhaps Jesus urges flight for that very reason.

Some of what Jesus says in this chapter could be about both the end times and the destruction of Jerusalem. Some is about one or the other. Early church fathers declared that these references in Matthew 24 are specifically about the events of AD 70.

Jesus already gave the disciples a list of things to watch for in anticipation of the end of the age. After the apocalyptic verse 29 reminiscent of Joel's prophecy, in verse 30 he answers their question about the sign of his coming. He will appear in the sky, all nations will see him and lament, he will gather his people from all points of the compass, horizon to horizon (see also Revelation 1:7.) He will be as visible as lightning and will come without warning.

Either we're living as if watching for his coming or not. Since we don't know exactly when it will be, readiness is essential and will be rewarded. Jesus' parable at the end of the chapter underscores that.

The hour of Christ's coming is known to God alone. It will be as sudden as a drenching summer deluge. It will entail judgment and separation. Inattention and procrastination will court tragedy. But we can be confident that faithfulness will count as we watch for him.

'I Wish We'd All Been Ready'

'Therefore keep watch, because you do not know the day or the hour' (v. 13).

Jesus' Olivet discourse continues. His three parables in chapter 25 emphasise faithfulness. The setting for the first is a wedding. Weddings involved the whole community and festivities lasted for several days. Jesus' first miracle took place at a wedding feast.

Wedding customs included the parents of the couple making a legal agreement, the bridegroom and friends visiting the bride's house and then the wedding party returning to the bridegroom's house. The marriage feast was the ceremony's finale.

The parable in today's passage refers to the second part – the processions. Even though they don't know exactly when he'll come, the bridesmaids who wait to meet the groom plan to welcome him as he comes for his bride. They doze, then nod off to sleep. The herald of the bridegroom's approach startles them awake in the middle of the night.

They all bring lamps for the night-time procession, but only some think to bring extra oil. As they try to turn up the lights, those without extra oil notice that their lamps are flickering out and ask the others for oil. The prepared refuse to diminish their needed supply, but suggest how those caught out might get more.

There are many believers who have some spiritual light, but untended it is faint or fading. We have to live by our own faith in Christ. God gives his grace to individuals. It empowers and attracts but it is not transferable, we each need to regularly secure our own supply from God. Believers know the means of grace accessible in Jesus' day are still available, chiefly through Scripture, prayer, worship, self-denial and simplicity of lifestyle for the gospel's sake.

This parable may be directed against the unpreparedness of the Jews who should have known the Messiah would come. More broadly, it speaks of the offer of salvation. It also foreshadows Jesus' own coming for his bride, the Church, and of the marriage supper of the Lamb (Revelation 19:6–9). There will be a final day. It's up to those invited to stay ready for his certain coming.

Entrusted

'His master replied, "Well done, good and faithful servant! You have been faithful with a few things; I will put you in charge of many things. Come and share your master's happiness!"' (v. 23).

Jesus' parable in Matthew 25 uses basic financial terms. A man is going abroad and entrusts three servants with three different amounts of silver according to what he thinks they can handle on his behalf in his absence. Two set to work investing the money. The third buries it.

The two who faithfully look after what is entrusted to them and return it doubled are commended, rewarded with more responsibility and invited to share the master's joy. The one who receives the least and returns it without any increase is condemned and loses out.

In a day when the stock market and even some banks aren't as reliable as we once thought, we might sympathise with the one who doesn't invest his silver. His only effort is digging a hole. His action is motivated by the thought that his master might not return. If he does return, the servant can return the initial amount without loss. But if the master doesn't return, the servant can keep the money without facing scrutiny by banks or investment advisers who would know it isn't his.

William Barclay says that in the context of the day, the useless servant stands for the scribes and Pharisees and their attitude toward things of God. They intend to keep things as they are. They can't tolerate any challenge.

But there are further lessons to take from the parable. People differ in ability and temperament. God suits different gifts to each. We are expected to use what we have in his service. A job well done begets more responsibility.

The crime of the one in the story who fails the test is that he makes no effort for his master's sake and considers only himself. As with any skills, only those who exercise them keep them.

———

To ponder:

How am I involved in serving the King as I wait for his return? What has he entrusted to me to manage on his behalf?

Kind or Cold?

'The King will reply, "I tell you the truth, whatever you did for one of the least of these brothers of mine, you did for me"' (v. 40).

Jesus finishes his teaching on the Mount of Olives with one more parable. This one deals with faithfulness in a third area – compassion. Instead of using commerce or ceremonies as the setting, this time he compares the King's coming judgment to a shepherd separating his sheep from his goats.

We think of sheep and goats as distinct. Goats have beards, sheep do not. Male sheep horns usually curl, goats' are straight. Yet sheep and goats share a number of characteristics. Both graze and chew their cud, have permanent horns and are surefooted. Only a trained eye can distinguish some wild varieties.

Surely only supernatural insight could distinguish between the 'sheep and goats' in Jesus' parable. The image in verse 33 is that of lining the animals up in rows extending out at the King's left and right sides. Here the King's judgment isn't based on what our society prizes – position, fame, wealth, wit, beauty, brawn, bravado – but on how we respond to human need. The things Jesus highlights are things anyone can do.

There's no special training required to offer food and drink to someone who needs it. We don't have to go far from where we live, or be part of an immense scheme, to participate in providing such basic aid. Opportunities to do so will frequently present themselves. We can also give and pray to empower those who are serving others in famine-ravaged lands.

Jesus' story shows that it is kindness that comes from loving hearts, not cunning minds, that counts. William Barclay reminds us: 'It is still true that there are those who will help if they are given praise and thanks and publicity; but to help like that is not to help, it is to pander to self-esteem. Such help is not generosity; it is disguised selfishness. The help which wins the approval of God is that which is given for nothing but the sake of helping.'[3]

This inasmuch serving is considered as serving Christ himself. Let's pray that the Holy Spirit will open our eyes to our opportunities and our hearts to showing generous kindness today.

In Conclusion

'As you know, the Passover is two days away – and the Son of Man will be handed over to be crucified' (v. 2).

Jesus finishes his Olivet talk. As he and the disciples make their way to Bethany, he reminds them again about his coming death. This time he doesn't talk about a future event but directly discloses imminent events set to start in two days. This time the Gospel writers don't record any reaction or protest from the disciples. Perhaps they are stunned, burdened or resigned.

Meanwhile, the Jewish leadership meets at the high priest's court and conspires to put Jesus to death in a sly way. The plan is to arrest Jesus after Passover, when the hordes of pilgrims have left Jerusalem. There are likely to be more than a million extra people in the city for the festival.

When the Jews commemorate their exodus from Egypt, fervour could easily ignite trouble. A riot could erupt. Caiaphas has been high priest for more than a dozen years. That's quite a record for an office that the Romans were accustomed to change frequently to suit their purposes. No doubt he wants to keep his position. Disposing of Jesus quietly after the holidays seems best.

God's plan moves forward toward its climax. After the incident of Jesus' anointing in Bethany (vv. 6–13), Judas makes himself available to betray Christ for profit. He offers to deliver Jesus to the chief priests for a fee, covertly, in line with their method. The tragedy unfolds.

Perhaps Judas is offended at Jesus' support of the woman's extravagant gift and mild rebuke to the disciples. Maybe Judas realises there won't be an earthly kingdom. Possibly money becomes Judas' incentive to cash in on what seems inevitable now – Jesus' death. Whatever his motive, Judas initiates the betrayal.

He receives pre-payment in silver for his work. It's both the price of a slave and the amount prophesied in Zechariah. Then he watches for his opportunity to betray Jesus and enable the Sanhedrin's plot. Who better than an insider to know the Master's movements well enough to assure success? Yet Jesus never shuts selfish Judas out. Judas does that himself. Free choice is a grave gift. We abuse it and refuse Christ at our peril.

The Cost of Loving

'I tell you the truth, wherever this gospel is preached throughout the world, what she has done will also be told, in memory of her' (v. 13).

Jesus' anointing at Bethany is told by Matthew, Mark and John. Luke tells a similar story with notable differences. It may have been of an earlier occurrence that inspired the incident he reported. John tells us that here the woman was Mary, sister of Martha and Lazarus.

Privately and forthrightly, Jesus several times tells his disciples of his death. They don't know how to handle his disclosures. But Mary does.

In response to the disciples' objections to the cost of her gift, Jesus avows that what she did is in preparation for his burial. She believes him. It is more than woman's intuition. Who better than the contemplative sister of Lazarus whom Jesus raised from the tomb to comprehend the certainty of Jesus' impending death?

Mary gives Jesus the most precious thing she owns and only he understands her heart's reasons and accepts the gift graciously.

The value of the fragrant ointment is nearly a year's wages – more than enough to feed 5,000 people. Ironically, this happens in Bethany, which means 'house of the poor'. Little wonder that the disciples are incensed. For Judas it is the tipping point. His subsequent choices cost him his life.

United Nations Day is observed on 24 October each year and One World Week is observed in the same week. Many use these times to consider ways to bridge cultures or challenge inequality and degradation locally and globally. We read statistics on the disparity in the cost of living and available resources around the world. The cost of *loving* isn't as measurable. Yet Mary's single gift of love is known around the world, as Jesus said it would be.

It's quite individual and personal. If we ask him, God will help us to know what our cost of loving should be.

To ponder:

What will I do for Jesus' sake?

Gifts

'For it is by grace you have been saved, through faith – and this not from yourselves, it is the gift of God' (v. 8).

Mary's Moment (Matthew 26:6–13)

Crouched in the corner of Simon's house
like a hollow, cast-off urn
holding only the dust of dreams,
she waits.

Something shining in his eyes
wrenches her captive heart.
Why do they offer him no wine,
no bread?

Tears born of uncommon love,
fall like rain on his feet,
and her desert of dying dreams
blossoms.

Marlene Chase

The Gift Exchange (John 1:14, 10:29)

He – God's gift to us,
wrapped in crimson pain,
in tears and sweat
and glory.
'The only Begotten – full of grace
and truth.'

We – God's gift to Jesus,
wrapped in scarlet sin,
in doubt and fear
and wonder.
Chosen children, bought by love
and grace!

Marlene Chase[4]

Anyone

Introduction

These days we don't carry flasks of fragrance to express our Christian faith. Told just prior to his anointing in Bethany, Jesus' parable of the sheep and goats suggests many practical ways of helping others in his name. The things Jesus highlights are things anyone can do.

Well before mobile phones, text messaging, voice mail, email, Post-it® notes or computers, Lieutenant-Colonel Mina Russell wrote a series of 'Anywoman' thoughts to help us seize daily opportunities to share our faith. For a few days we'll share excerpts from her series. I have adapted some of her 'Anywoman' pieces to be 'Anyman' as well.

She frames her thoughts in everyday activities such as cooking, driving, reading, visiting, writing, keeping silent and giving prayer prompts. If we want to look for opportunities and are ready to share our faith, we will discover openings to apply her straightforward lessons in fresh ways.

Consider reading the Scripture passage from Matthew 25 in a different version each day.

Lieutenant-Colonel Mina Russell was a Bible teacher, specialist on prayer and effective counsellor who taught at Brengle (holiness) Institutes organised by The Salvation Army around the world. Much of that was in her retirement. During active service, she spent many years on the New York training college staff. She was admitted to the Order of the Founder, the highest Salvation Army honour for distinguished service such as would in spirit or achievement have been specially commended by the Army's Founder, William Booth.

Through Making Jam

'Inasmuch as ye have done it unto one of the least of these my brethren,
ye have done it unto me' (v. 40, KJV).

'Anywoman' was a good cook. Everyone knew it. Not only were her pies and cakes excellent, but her pot roast, and baked chicken were 'tops'. She had another skill along this line which was seasonal. She could make jam. Each year as summer neared its end, she would begin. The house was filled with special aromas that made everyone wish it was time to eat the delicious 'whatever-it-was'.

Anywoman used her time well so that her house was not upset by such activities. One day it would be a few baskets of berries, another day a few pounds of peaches. It was never a full-scale operation that disturbed the household's routine, but somehow the cupboard filled up with her handiwork, a winter's supply.

Jam season gave Anywoman special joy. She knew that all good things came from God, including fruits. If money should be tithed, so should other gifts. This meant her jams. There were always people who could not do what she did with fruit. There were shut-ins for whom a jar of jam would mean a little joy on a dark day.

When she went on her excursions she kept her little gift hidden. Usually the information came out later: 'Your mother makes the best jam.' And she did.

Anywoman discounted her generosity. She was sharing what God had provided. She was just a homemaker, not an evangelist; but when she flavoured her jams with love and prayers, they conveyed the message and became the medium for showing her love and sharing her faith.

When she died her tribute included: 'She lived a full life, but without trappings of ostentation. With reserve and sympathy and dignity she strove for the ultimate purpose of the organisation in which she laboured: the salvation of the person, the ministering to the needs of the individual and family. In doing her full share to accomplish this, she naturally contributed to the improvement of the community as a whole.' Anywoman was a Christian.

To ponder:

Couldn't any woman do the same?

Through Driving

*'Whenever you did one of these things to someone overlooked or ignored,
that was me – you did it to me' (v. 40, MSG).*

'Anyman' has a car. Although he bought it himself, he thinks of it as a gift from God. It's another evidence of God's goodness to him. He is no longer young and may have to stop driving one day, but not yet. The way he feels about the car and uses it could mean many more years of service for others.

When he knew that he would be living near a home for seniors, he got an idea, an inspiration. He made inquiries and found that he could take some of the residents on trips to shops. It seemed like a good idea, so the residence posted a notice that on a certain day he would be available to take a few passengers on short trips. The space for the names of those interested soon filled, so requests were made for later dates. This is how it started.

Anyman continues to do this week after week. The day he sets aside for this purpose is not his to use in any other way except under the most unusual circumstances. That day is his gift to others given in the spirit and name of Christ. It seems so little when he thinks of what God has given him through the years.

Many people say, 'Let me know when you want to go shopping and I'll take you.' And that is where it ends. Others tell the residence manager that they would like to help some time. But Anyman made a plan, stated a time and type of service he could offer, and now he provides the service.

He enjoys the trips too. Even when his passengers don't return with purchases, he knows they have had a good time on their outing. It could be that the warm, happy conversations are important parts of the afternoon. The fact that someone cares and shares his car and his attention underlies the pleasure they receive.

Possibly his passengers know why he does it – to share his faith and exhibit Christian love.

To ponder:

Do you have a car? Could you share your faith by using it as a gift from God for others?

Through Reading

'Whenever you did it for any of my people, no matter how unimportant
they seemed, you did it for me' (v. 40, CEV).

'Anywoman' lived close to a veterans' hospital and was glad to volunteer her services there. Yet she wondered what she could offer the men and women who had served their country.

The chaplain suggested several things. One was visiting the long-term and elderly patients who sometimes faced empty futures. Anywoman visited the women's floor and generally received a warm response to her visits. But one woman was especially unhappy. Everything was wrong. No one cared and she didn't either. It would be good for everyone if she died.

This was Anywoman's opportunity. She visited the woman regularly. She asked if the woman had a favourite author. When she mentioned a title, Anywoman looked for it. She read to the patient who seemed to enjoy it. Anywoman always finished her visits with a prayer and hoped her friend might come to know peace with God and with herself.

One afternoon was less than successful. Anywoman's cheerful greeting was met with, 'No reading today. Just pray and go.' That is what Anywoman did. There were other more satisfactory visits.

Anywoman would have been happy if she could have known that her patient had accepted Christ before she died. She did not know, but she remembered that in the hours they spent together, God often seemed to be near with a healing, comforting touch. She would have to leave the ultimate judgment to God who can heal a person's spirit at a depth no one else can touch.

Anywoman was glad she'd given time to a person who could no longer hold a book. They had read the patient's choice, *The Life of Christ*, together.

To ponder:

It is possible that you can find someone with whom to share your faith through visiting and reading. There are others who cannot hold a book and some who cannot see to read.

Through Writing

'When you did it to one of the least of these my brothers and sisters,
you were doing it to me' (v. 40, NLT).

'Anywoman' never felt able to write a story for a magazine. In fact, writing anything didn't often fit into her schedule through the years. That didn't mean she didn't enjoy reading what others wrote.

One day Anywoman heard that the mother of a friend had died. How do you let someone know how you feel at a time like this? Flowers didn't seem the answer. Perhaps money could be sent with a sympathy card. The cards with their lovely verses and flowers expressed concern, but just weren't right this time.

Anywoman prayed that there would be a way adequately to express sympathy. The next day the idea came to write a letter and let God guide her words. She remembered what happened when a loved one died. There were endless discussions, decisions, telephone calls, notes to write, plans to make.

So Anywoman wrote:

These days will be difficult for you and you will be very busy with many things to think about. It will seem that everything has to be done at once. People must be notified and plans made on the spot. You may find that you have no time to pray and you may not feel like praying when you do have a few minutes. If this is so, don't worry about it. Just go on doing what needs to be done and know that I will be praying for you. I know God will help you and you will feel the warmth of my love and faith, which I will send to you through God.

That was about all. Anywoman sealed the envelope with a sense that God had guided the words and they would help a bit. And they did help. When the letter arrived, the friend knew that Anywoman understood and would be praying. Other messages arrived as well, but the words of Anywoman with a promise of prayer seemed to undergird her.

The message was simple, but because Anywoman shared faith through the letter, the prayer would give needed strength for those days. The letter is still remembered and it is the way any woman can share faith and serve the Lord with gladness.

Through Silence

*'Assuredly, I say to you, inasmuch as you did it to one of the least
of these my brethren, you did it to me' (v. 40, NKJV).*

It was the worst story about a person 'Anyman' had ever heard. It was shocking, surprising and very sad. He felt that a great tree had fallen when the news came and he wondered how he could help. He wanted to defend the person. It just couldn't be true, and yet there was evidence that something was wrong. He prayed that God would minister to the hurting.

It was logical for someone to bring up the subject because he knew the person well. He was glad nothing was said at first because he couldn't believe it was true. He really didn't know what he would say if someone had mentioned it.

Then it happened. A friend said, 'Why didn't you tell me the big news about so-and-so?' Anyman looked at him and replied, 'I'm not talking about it. I only know what I've heard and there may be more to it. If it is true, it's too tragic to discuss. If it's not true, it will be forgotten.'

There was an awkward silence. Then the conversation went to other matters. Later Anyman felt he had done the only thing he could. He was glad he had turned off the subject quickly.

The friend thought about it too and felt it was an effective way to deal with gossip. If you keep silent, you break the chain of talk and help the rumours to die. If you talk about it, you help perpetuate it. The way Anyman handled it seemed wise.

The friend remembered the lesson. Years later when they talked together, the friend who asked the question reminded him of that conversation and said, 'Whatever you knew about it remained with you. There was no gossip that day.'

Anyman was glad, but remembered other times when he'd joined right in with the talk and felt ashamed he had not always been kind and wise. He knew how he would act in the future. Gossip would stop with him. Nothing would be passed along. It might be difficult to keep quiet, but it would be worth it if it broke the chain of hurtful talk. It would be a way to share his faith.

———————

To ponder:

Can't anyone do this?

Through Daily Reminders

'I assure you that whatever you did for the humblest of my
brothers you did for me' (v. 40, JBP).

'Anywoman' was in her teens when she was converted in The Salvation Army. She was rather shy and reserved, but took her place as a member and attended meetings regularly. When she married, her home became a Christian home. Grace was said before meals, and Bible reading and prayer shared after meals.

As their children grew they were taught to pray simple prayers, then the Lord's Prayer at bedtime. But Anywoman decided this was not enough for her children. They should pray to start the day. It was during the day that they met temptations and problems. So she began daily reminders.

Morning was difficult. Someone would stay in bed too long and need extra help to be ready for school on time. One of the four would be ill and need extra attention. The clock moved too fast and the children's friends were waiting for them outside. Anywoman developed a habit that annoyed her children.

As they went out the door she would ask them, 'Have you prayed this morning?' Often the answer was, 'I'm late.' Anywoman showed unusual determination, commanding, 'Come back here and pray before you go.' And they did.

Some would feel that such prayer wasn't much of a prayer. Perhaps it wasn't, but it planted the seeds of a lifetime habit which was reinforced. Anywoman wondered if she was doing the right thing when she made prayer compulsory. But her children remember her daily reminders. 'Begin the day with God' has been meaningful in their lives.

Anywoman reminded her children to depend on God to make the days what they ought to be. She didn't think it was a dramatic way of sharing her faith, but the reminders weren't forgotten.

Any woman could help her children establish a pattern for life by asking such questions.

———————

To ponder:

How do we remember what's important to us? What can I use to incorporate spiritual truths and prompts for prayer in my daily routine?

For All the Saints

'Our God comes and will not be silent' (v. 3).

For those who sense autumn's walk toward winter . . . 'November':

> Sweet stillness of grey November.
> Leaves, like trailing glory clouds,
> settle, stir, die and bury
> to wait a slow rebirth. We live in
> November – this poor dying time,
> but April comes, inexorable, sudden,
> when we shall live more nobly and well.
> Still, this lingering is sweet.
> Precious the grey November
> and every memory of April past,
> every thought of April to come.
> Precious – for every moment in life and death
> God is awake.

For those who see springtime's dance toward summer . . . 'Royal Treasures':

> Fire blazing on the hill,
> embers lining clouds
> crimson, silver, gold
> God's treasures counted,
> extravagantly spilled.
> He could have chosen
> to recall his fiery star
> in discreet silence.
> Instead he gifts the world
> with mighty sunsets, feasts
> for famished souls.
> We go on our way refreshed,
> reminded we are kings
> and queens and richly loved –
> oh, so richly loved!

Both poems are from the pen of Marlene Chase.

In Remembrance

We remember people in many ways. Countries erect statues or name buildings to keep names and deeds of national heroes in the public consciousness from generation to generation. We see sculptures of prominent religious leaders, too. The enduring quality of bronze or stone suggests permanency. Benefactors endow institutions, projects or prizes to ensure their names continue to be remembered.

Some who don't strive for repute are still remembered by those they benefited, be they many or few. We think of modest sites that serve as memorials to outstanding ministers of the gospel. There are tributes on websites, in church publications and newspapers.

We have recently considered the lives and deaths of Sarah and Abraham. When his wife died, Abraham purchased a burial cave. It was a place of both mourning and remembrance (Genesis 23 and 25).

At various times of the year people pause to remember those who have died. Many cultures include memorial meetings, sometimes at cemeteries or memorial parks. Although the customs surrounding death vary around the world, the desire to respectfully remember is universal.

We will share some thoughts from a place of remembrance. Kensico Cemetery in the hamlet of Valhalla, within the town of Mount Pleasant, New York, USA, was founded in 1889. It followed the American plan for landscaped cemeteries begun sixty years earlier. Kensico takes its name from a local Native American chief of the 1700s. Although there are notables buried throughout the 461 acres, The Salvation Army section is of particular interest. We will focus on some of its memorials that quote Scripture. (For the list of the hundreds of inscriptions – not names – collected, email Evelyn.Merriam@use.salvationarmy.org)

Abraham's tomb filled up, as have many tombs, catacombs, cemeteries and places of remembrance through the ages. We thank God for his faithful ones. But we rejoice most of all that Jesus' tomb is empty! His resurrection is a foundation of our faith: 'Praise be to the God and Father of our Lord Jesus Christ! In his great mercy he has given us new birth into a living hope through the resurrection of Jesus Christ from the dead' (1 Peter 1:3).

What Do These Stones Mean?

*'And Joshua set up at Gilgal the twelve stones they had
taken out of the Jordan' (v. 20).*

When the Israelites finally crossed the Jordan River into the Promised Land, their leader, Joshua, instructed them to erect stones in memory of their crossing and prompt their descendants to ask questions and learn about God's faithfulness.

We visit The Salvation Army section of Kensico Cemetery. The hundreds of memorial stones teach us about the lives and faith of some notable, and many more ordinary, saints. I walk through the Army section where the majority of the headstones face east. I methodically record just the inscriptions, but not names. Believers' names are more permanently written in the Book of Life, I muse.

I note the brief memorial descriptions. Besides the more typical choices, my collection includes plenty of unique inscriptions too – 'Salvationist zealot', 'complete in Christ', 'a woman of prayer', 'mission accomplished Acts 16:31 to the third generation', 'dance unto the Lord', 'a herald of victory', 'his "second miles" would circle the world', 'pioneer slum officer', 'a valiant lady', 'white unto harvest', 'Christian gentleman' and 'I walk with the King, Hallelujah'.

Phrases reflect themes of peace, faith, grace, service, character and faithfulness. There are many references to music and excerpts from songs. The majority of inscriptions are scriptural. We'll consider a few of these in the next days.

Visiting such a place reminds us of what the writer of Hebrews calls a 'great cloud of witnesses'. Memorial stones can be inspirational. Joshua was right: they can testify to the Lord's power and stir us to worship him.

———————

To ponder:

What would I want an inscription to say of my life and my faith?

The Shepherd's Own

'And I will dwell in the house of the LORD forever' (v. 6).

There are many types of memorials. One of the most personal is a grave marker. If the grave marker's inscription is chosen by the deceased, it may be a testimony. If chosen by others, it may be a way of remembering the loved one. It could be a single word, part of a song or a description of a life's focus or service.

Hundreds of the headstones in well-tended, landscaped Kensico Cemetery feature a verse of Scripture. Psalm 23 appears a number of times. One headstone from 1921 says: 'The major's last words, "Yea, though I walk through the valley of the shadow of death I will fear no evil for thou art with me, thy rod and thy staff they comfort me." That's enough. That will do.'

More poignant for me is the simple statement of faith on the headstone of a single woman who lived to age ninety-nine, Lieutenant-Colonel Mina Russell. She was on the planning commission for the first Brengle (holiness) Institute. After forty-three years of Christian service, she continued to travel around the world to teach about prayer and practical holiness for nearly another twenty years in retirement.

Many could have suggested lofty epitaphs in her memory, but she chose, 'The LORD is my shepherd.' Even through her headstone she simply and eloquently continues to point us to the God she loved and served.

Hymnwriter William Walsham How writes:

> For all the saints who from their labours rest,
> Who thee by faith before the world confessed,
> Thy name, O Jesus, be forever blessed,
> Hallelujah! Hallelujah!
>
> But lo! there breaks a yet more glorious day:
> The saints triumphant rise in bright array;
> The King of Glory passes on his way,
> Hallelujah! Hallelujah!

Faithful

*'Be faithful, even to the point of death, and I will give
you the crown of life' (v. 10).*

Today's verse is another popular one at Kensico. Besides derivatives of the verse, a score of stones reflect faithfulness to God, duty, family or friends. General Edward Higgins' marker states: 'He faltered not but served his God faithfully to the end'.

One was written by General Evangeline Booth of her secretary for forty years, Lieutenant-Commissioner Richard Griffith: 'Faithful devoted soldier of the cross and flag – valiant in the performance of deeds in advance of and beyond his duty'. Just as articulate are the seven stones with the single resilient word, 'Faithful'. Perhaps it recalls someone who quietly served the Lord for many years through varied circumstances. But faithfulness doesn't have a minimum duration requirement. Neither does it come in degrees. Either one is faithful to a leader or a mission or not.

If a marathon runner, mountain climber or missionary dies while doing something they love, although the circumstances may seem tragic, we often consider them fortunate to have been actively engaged and fully alive. They were faithful to their treasured undertaking to the end, however long they had.

Two years ago Colonel Bo Brekke, a Salvation Army officer from Norway who had served in six territories in Europe and South Asia, was killed. That week General Shaw Clifton said of the colonel and his wife:

> Their concern for the poor and marginalised, their giftedness in lifting up the downtrodden, their loving hearts have resulted in countless lives transformed from penury to dignity and many coming to faith in Jesus. When Bo was killed he and Birgitte were serving as the leaders of The Salvation Army in Pakistan. They took risks in order to be available to others, in obedience to the commands of Christ. Bo lived and died for others.

Another verse of William Walsham How's hymn, 'For All The Saints', declares:

> Thou wast their rock, their fortress and their might;
> Thou, Lord, their captain in the well-fought fight;
> Thou in the darkness drear their one true light,
> Hallelujah! Hallelujah!

In His Presence

*'Glory and honour are in his presence; strength and gladness
are in his place' (1 Chronicles 16:27).*

On my walk through Kensico I note the inscription 'In his presence' only once. Part of the final verse of today's psalm appears twice: 'in thy presence is fullness of joy' (Psalm 16:11, *KJV*). Elizabeth Swift Brengle's inscription, 'My Lord, with thee', is in the same vein. Believers will experience the joy of living in God's presence eternally in heaven. But we can know a foretaste of it now. Songwriters have described the blessing and how to obtain it:

> All to Jesus I surrender, all to him I freely give;
> I will ever love and trust him, in his presence daily live.
> *Judson Van de Venter (SASB 474)*

> In the love of Jesus there is all I need,
> While I follow closely where my Lord may lead;
> By his grace forgiven, in his presence blest,
> In the love of Jesus, in the love of Jesus, is perfect rest.
> *Ivy Mawby (SASB 740)*

> Now daily the Saviour is showing
> How gracious his presence can be;
> The life which he promised is growing
> And finding fulfilment in me.
> Engaged in his sacred employment
> And furnished with all that I need,
> In him I have fullest enjoyment,
> In him perfect friendship indeed.
> *Will J. Brand (SASB 553)*

> In your presence there is comfort,
> In your presence there is peace.
> When we seek to know your heart,
> We will find such blessed assurance
> In your holy presence, Lord.
> *Dick and Melodie Tunney*[5]

71

Do, Love, Walk

'But he's already made it plain how to live, what to do, what God is looking for in men and women. It's quite simple: Do what is fair and just to your neighbour, be compassionate and loyal in your love, And don't take yourself too seriously – take God seriously' (v.8, MSG).

The *King James Version* of today's verse appears several times on stones set in the rows between Lakeview and Tecumseh Avenues at Kensico. At one site it becomes a tribute. Mrs General Catherine Higgins' stone says: 'She did justly, loved mercy and walked humbly with her God'.

In Micah's day the sacrificial system was an outward expression of inner obedience to God and faith in his grace. The prophet asks if burnt offerings, yearling calves, countless rams, rivers of oil or even the sacrifice of a firstborn child could gain his people entrance into God's favour and atone for their sin. His rhetorical question stresses that nothing Israel could offer would be enough.

Rituals aren't the answer. They need a change of heart and an attitude of voluntary dependence on God. Micah says God mercifully provides a way. It involves treating others fairly, meeting the needs of others lovingly and loyally and living in fellowship with God respectfully and unpretentiously.

One part leads into the next. Acting justly toward God, others and self leads to loving mercy. Loving mercy means going beyond what justice requires and doing what kindness and love entail. Living this way doesn't earn salvation but evidences knowledge of a personal need for God's saving mercy. Only the redeemed can truly know the pleasure of walking humbly with their God.

Two other memorial inscriptions seem apt with today's thoughts. One was written first of Jesus: 'He went about doing good for God was with him'. The other declares: 'He walked with God'.

To ponder:

> How wonderful it is to walk with God
> Along the road that holy men have trod;
> How wonderful it is to hear him say:
> Fear not, have faith, 'tis I who lead the way!
> *Theodore Hopkins Kitching* (*SASB* 583)

What's in His Hands?

*'In his hand are the depths of the earth, and the mountain
peaks belong to him' (v. 4).*

We see the word 'hand' in the Bible hundreds of times. Many times it is used literally, but many more times figuratively, mostly referring to God's hand.

Ecclesiastes 5:15 reminds us that we are born with nothing in our hands and carry nothing away from this life in our hands. But during our lives we use our hands moment by moment. Sometimes the Lord reminds us of, or directs us to use, what is in our hands for his purposes. He often prospers the work of our hands. When a matter is given into someone's hand, it is turned over to their care.

Something that God's hand accomplishes refers to his power and authority. His 'strong hand' delivered Israel from Egypt. He used his hands to make the heavens and earth (v. 5). God sustains and directs the righteous by his hand (Psalm 139:10).

Several times in the Old Testament we see the Lord with an instrument of measurement in his hand. In the New Testament he holds an implement of harvest, whether for threshing or reaping. Both speak of judgment.

The *King James Version* states today's verse: 'In his hand are the deep places of the earth: the strength of the hills is his also.' A missionary told me she found that verse reassuring as she thought of her mother's burial thousands of miles away.

Several grey granite stones at Kensico give a name and the simple epitaph, 'In his hands'. The words were most likely chosen from Salvationist songwriter Stanley E. Ditmer's assuring chorus, 'I'm in his hands'. Let it remind us of God's providential care:

> I'm in his hands, I'm in his hands;
> Whate'er the future holds
> I'm in his hands,
> The days I cannot see
> Have all been planned for me;
> His way is best, you see;
> I'm in his hands.
>
> (*SASB* 732)

Living Memorials

*'They are living memorials to show that the Lord is upright
and faithful to his promises; He is my rock, and there is no
unrighteousness in Him' (v. 15, AB).*

In some places today is Remembrance Sunday. This is in addition to the observance of Remembrance Day on 11 November. Among other things, moments of silence are included in church services today. It is also the International Day of Prayer for the Persecuted Church. Whether we remember those who sacrificed their lives during war or those who are persecuted for their faith, it is a day of remembering.

And it is a day for determining to be living memorials for God. Charles Spurgeon said: 'A good character is the best tombstone. Those who loved you and were helped by you will remember you when forget-me-nots have withered. Carve your name on hearts, not on marble.' We say, Amen.

Psalm 92 is called a song for the Sabbath day.

> It is good to praise the LORD
> > and make music to your name, O Most High,
> to proclaim your love in the morning
> > and your faithfulness at night,
> to the music of the ten-stringed lyre
> > and the melody of the harp.
> For you make me glad by your deeds, O LORD;
> > I sing for joy at the works of your hands.
> How great are your works, O LORD,
> > how profound your thoughts! . . .
> The righteous will flourish like a palm tree,
> > they will grow like a cedar of Lebanon;
> planted in the house of the LORD,
> > they will flourish in the courts of our God.
> They will still bear fruit in old age,
> > they will stay fresh and green,
> proclaiming, 'The LORD is upright;
> > he is my Rock, and there is no wickedness in him.

Paradoxes and Promises

'Blessed are those whose strength is in you, who have set their hearts on pilgrimage' (v. 5).

Several inscriptions focus on strength. One uses a variation of Nehemiah 8:10 and testifies: 'The joy of the Lord is *my* strength'.

After they'd rebuilt the walls of Jerusalem, when the people heard Ezra read God's Word for the first time they wept. Nehemiah encouraged the tens of thousands gathered to think of the day as specially blessed rather than as a time to weep. Their leaders urged them to share food with each other and rejoice in the Lord who was their strength. Holiness and joy were partners.

The priests reinforced the message that the day was holy and the people should be still, but not sad. The idea that stillness or quietness can be a spring of strength is a paradox we find in other places in Scripture.

Several memorial stones bear witness with part of another verse: 'In returning and rest shall ye be saved; in quietness and in confidence shall be your strength' (Isaiah 30:15, *KJV*). Another inscription is again from Isaiah: 'But they that wait upon the LORD shall renew their strength' (40:13, *KJV*).

What is the source of such strength? Today's verse from Psalm 84 reminds us that it is God. We followers of Christ who recognise our complete dependence on the Lord can travel toward heaven with hope, even when we pass through the valley of weeping (v. 6). As yet another inscription asserts: 'They go from strength to strength till we appear before God' (v. 7).

Finally, an etched verse encourages us: 'As thy days, so shall thy strength be' (Deuteronomy 33:25, *KJV*). We need reminders of such promises.

To ponder:

In my life, how can joy and strength be co-workers? How can quietness and confidence be partners? Thank God for being your strength for today.

Witnesses from the Word

'For the word of God is living and active' (Hebrews 4:12).

Walk thoughtfully past the grey granite stones and notice many of the other verses of Scripture carved in memorial at Kensico. Most are from the *King James Version*. Some use just a reference, but the following verses appear written out. We'll let them speak for themselves:

A building of God eternal in the heavens; More than conquerors; I have chosen you; His way is perfect; Free from the law of sin and death; And their works do follow them; Present with the Lord; Her children call her blessed; Surely I come quickly. Amen. Even so, come Lord Jesus; Love never faileth; So faith, hope, love abide, but the greatest of these is love; He asked life of thee and thou gavest it him even length of days forever and ever; Victory through our Lord Jesus Christ; A workman that needeth not to be ashamed; Who shall separate us from the love of Christ?

But as it is written, eye hath not seen, nor ear heard, neither have entered into the heart of man, the things which God hath prepared for them that love him; Let her own works praise her in the gates; I was in prison and ye visited me; To him be all the glory; And they loved not their lives unto the death; And in the stone a new name written; Joy cometh in the morning; Because I live, ye shall live also; The name of the Lord is a strong tower the righteous runneth into it and is safe; Called, chosen, faithful; Above rubies; This one thing I do; Seek ye first the kingdom; Thy kingdom come, thy will be done; The eternal God is her refuge; Under the shadow of the almighty.

Whosoever liveth and believeth in me shall never die; He bringeth them into their desired haven; Holding forth the word of life; Blessed are the pure in heart; Steadfast, unmoveable, always abounding; Neither count I my life dear unto myself so that I might finish my course with joy; They overcame; Till the morning breaks and shadows flee away; By his stripes I am healed; I will lift up mine eyes unto the hills, from whence cometh my help; In thee, O Lord, do I put my trust; Blessed are the dead which die in the Lord; Death is swallowed up in victory; Whatever you do, do heartily, as unto the Lord; For thou are greatly beloved; He that doeth the will of God abideth forever; Emmanuel.

Remembrancers

'Then those who feared the LORD talked with each other, and the LORD listened and heard. A scroll of remembrance was written in his presence concerning those who feared the LORD and honoured his name' (v. 16).

Whether we call it Remembrance Day, Armistice Day, Poppy Day or Veterans Day, today is the anniversary of the end of the First World War in 1918. It is a day to commemorate the sacrifices of members of the armed forces and civilians in times of war.

Traditionally there is silence at the eleventh hour of the eleventh day of the eleventh month. In some places the primary observances are held on the second Sunday of November, Remembrance Sunday.

In the Old Testament, recorders or chroniclers of official or important events could have been called 'remembrancers'. They aided the collective memory. *Young's Literal Translation* and the *Amplified Bible* also use that word or concept for people who by their prayers remind the Lord of his promises (Isaiah 62:6).

When I studied Japanese I was told 'to remember' is not the same as 'not to forget'. The Greek in the New Testament makes that distinction as well. There is a subtle difference between remembering and not forgetting.

Not forgetting implies always keeping the person or thing in mind. Remembering speaks of being mindful again, of someone or something that may have slipped our minds. It may take another's prompting. If we need memory prompts to remind us of ordinary things, how much more essential it is of eternal things.

In some cases, caregivers or loved ones need to remember on behalf of one whose memory sporadically breaks down. Norwegian writer Arne Garborg said: 'To love a person is to learn the song that is in their heart and to sing it to them when they have forgotten.' Perhaps in a similar way we can be 'remembrancers' for the sake of others. It can be a privilege and vital ministry to pray for those who need to connect or reconnect with the Lord. Ask the Lord if there is someone you know who needs a 'remembrancer'.

It's a blessing to know someone is interceding for us, and that we are remembered. Most of all, we delight that God remembers those who reverence and honour him.

Fully Focused

Introduction

Colossians is one of Paul's Epistles to seven churches. It is one of the letters he wrote while imprisoned in Rome. He wrote the Epistles of Philemon, Ephesians and Colossians at about the same time.

The Colossian church was largely Gentile. It probably met at the home of a well-to-do believer, Philemon. Although Paul did not found the church in Colosse, its start no doubt emanated from his extensive ministry in Ephesus when 'all the Jews and Greeks who lived in the province of Asia heard the word of the Lord' (Acts 19:10). Colosse was located about 100 miles east of Ephesus.

Some readers consider that many of Paul's verses in Colossians resemble some in Ephesians. There may be similarities of expression, but with a different aim and emphasis. Ephesians is a book of doctrine. Colossians is a book of correction.

Here Paul points believers away from reliance on human-made rules and traditions to ethical oneness with Christ as the true mark of a Christian. The aim of his teaching is Christ-likeness. Paul begins with a greeting of grace and he finishes Colossians as he does all of his letters, with a prayer for God's grace.

To a Church in Sheep Country

'I greet the Christians and stalwart followers of Christ who live in Colosse. May everything good from God our Father be yours!' (v. 2, MSG)

Colosse is not on our maps today. During Paul's time it was a town in the Roman province of Asia. It included a significant Jewish population. For a time, Colosse's location allowed it to command the roads to mountain passes. It was one of three municipalities situated near the Lycus River in Phyrgia. Laodicaea continued to thrive as a political centre. Hierapolis prospered as a trade centre and hot spring spa.

The chalky river waters encrusted areas of the land, making them look like glaciers. Where there were chalk-free volcanic deposits, the ground was fertile. Large flocks of sheep thrived. Colosse developed a large wool industry. Laodicea produced quality garments. The chalky waters were good for dyeing cloth, so working together Laodicea and Colosse produced coloured wool which was highly prized and the basis of the economy.

For some reason, Colosse's status diminished. Not long after Paul wrote, the town is thought to have been destroyed by one of the earthquakes so prevalent in that volcanic area.

Paul had not visited the church in Colosse when he wrote this letter from his imprisonment in Rome. Some say it was the least important town to which Paul wrote a letter. Yet in this short letter Paul's Christology is at its height.

Paul starts with his qualification – an apostle. When he uses the particular word order for whose apostle he is, 'of Christ Jesus', he emphasises that Jesus is the Messiah. This is important, considering the issues Paul intends to address.

As he did in several letters, Paul says he writes with brother Timothy. One of Paul's converts is his equal in Christ. Although an apostle with special credentials and commission, Paul places himself as one among other Christian associates.

He writes to the holy and trustworthy followers of Christ in Colosse. Paul writes to the Colossian church, but doesn't address them as 'the church' as he does elsewhere, but as God's people in a specific place, Colosse. As we read this portion of God's word, let's ask God's Holy Spirit to speak specifically to us, his people, as well.

Possibility Prayer

'We always thank God, the Father of our Lord Jesus Christ,
when we pray for you' (v. 3).

It took us a little while to recognise it as a custom after we arrived in Japan. Besides the expected greeting, 'Good day, how are you?' acquaintances often added, 'Thank you for your recent kindness.' At first we tried to remember anything we might have said or done, but we soon found out that the proper response was, 'Not at all. I should be thanking you.' We learned to practise the custom.

That came to mind when I read today's Scripture. Paul follows his greeting of grace and peace to believers at Colosse with the fact that 'we' (presumably he and Timothy at least) always thank God in prayer for the Colossians' response to the gospel exhibited in their faith in God and their love for God's people.

This springs from their eternal hope in heaven which 'the word of truth', the gospel, brought them. Further he says he's thankful for the growth of the gospel in them as well as throughout the world. Then he folds in the one who brought the gospel to them, Epaphras, a fellow Christian servant and minister. He lets them know that since coming to Rome, Epaphras has told him good things about their love in the Spirit.

I can almost hear them protesting, 'Not at all. We should be thanking God for you.' If they haven't been praying for Paul, their own minister Epaphras and other Christian leaders, perhaps they begin even as they hear Paul's letter read aloud.

In verses 9–11 Paul prays for them that they will know God's will, seek his wisdom and live accordingly, empowered by his strength. Why? So they can bear suffering whatever they must face for God's glory; display patience with people's ungodly actions without succumbing to despair; and do it all with genuine resilient joy. On our own such a goal is impossible, but it is possible with God. It takes daily divine grace. Are we willing to seek the Holy Spirit's help today?

To pray:

'Make me, O Lord, victorious over every circumstance; make me patient with every person; and withal give me the joy which no circumstance and no man will ever take from me.'

William Barclay[6]

From Our Night to His Light

'God rescued us from dead-end alleys and dark dungeons' (v.13, MSG).

Paul introduces a theme he often uses with Gentile Christians. He reminds the Colossians that God transferred them from darkness to light. Salvation doesn't depend on access to special knowledge, as the Gnostics claim. We are redeemed from sin, brought into the kingdom of God's Son, to share in the inheritance of God's people. This is cause for heartfelt thanksgiving.

He contrasts their former condition of being alienated from God, even hostile toward things of God, with being reconciled to God. Paul emphasises that this was made possible through Christ's physical death. He wants to counter the Gnostic notion that Jesus did not have a tangible human body.

It is important to realise that Jesus wasn't pretending to be human or granting himself divine favours while he was on earth. He came to share our human frailties and weaknesses, and by doing so, he experienced death too. He was one of us and one with us.[7]

What is the aim of Christ's death for our reconciliation? Besides forgiveness of sin and acquittal from God's deserved judgment, Christ died that we could be holy, blameless people. Paul says that in response to what Christ has done for us, our part is to continue steadfastly in our faith and to hold on to our hope in the gospel.

The gospel the Colossians heard and believed was the same good news proclaimed everywhere; it was not a private faith available to a select group. It is the same gospel we embrace. By God's grace we receive it to live it and share it.

Paul urges continuance in the faith. He would not do so if it wasn't possible to be deceived and fall away. Our hope in the gospel, God's good news, is for the present as well as the future. It keeps us going now and informs us of wonderful things yet to come.

Songwriter John Gowans reminds us how compelling God's call from darkness to light, from winter to springtime in Christ really is:

> Out of my darkness he called me
> Into his sunshining day,
> Out of my gloom to his glory;
> What could I do but obey?
> (*SASB* 378)

81

Ancient Song

'Your attitude should be the same as that of Christ Jesus' (v. 5).

The early Church called Philippians 2:6–11 the *Carmen Christi* hymn to Christ. Christians used it to remind themselves of who Jesus is. It all turns on his obedience and the cross. In his *Scribbling in the Sand*,[8] songwriter and musician Michael Card says that verses six to eight of the ancient hymn would be in a minor key and nine to eleven in a major one:

> Here Lordship and exaltation are shown to be the unexpected results of humility and servanthood, all because of the empowering force of radical obedience! . . . This radical reversal is seen every time the kingdom breaks through . . . But, as he so often does, Paul has another purpose for his hymn . . . Just when we thought it was safe to sing this impersonal and incarnational song we glance at the introductory verse (Philippians 2:5) and discover that this pattern of Jesus' life is meant to be applied to our lives as well. We are to have the same attitude, Paul says!

> Who, being in very nature God,
>> did not consider equality with God something to be grasped,
> but made himself nothing,
>> taking the very nature of a servant,
>> being made in human likeness.
> And being found in appearance as a man,
>> he humbled himself
>> and became obedient to death – even death on a cross!
> Therefore God exalted him to the highest place
>> and gave him the name that is above every name,
> that at the name of Jesus every knee should bow,
>> in heaven and on earth and under the earth,
> and every tongue confess that Jesus Christ is Lord,
>> to the glory of God the Father.

All in All

'He is the image of the invisible God, the firstborn over all creation' (v. 15).

Jesus is the very image of God. The word Paul uses for image, *eikon*, is some-times used of wisdom in the Old Testament. So to Jews, Paul says: you revere the wisdom and goodness of God, it is Jesus who is that wisdom of God.

The same word is sometimes used interchangeably with *logos*, the rational word or mind of God. To the Greeks, who view this as essential and sacred, he says Jesus is that invisible divine image of God made visible.

Another use of the word for image is for a portrait or detailed description of a person. Today we might think of composites of our signatures, fingerprints, irises, DNA or vocal patterns for physical identification. Jesus is that composite 'biometric' of God's characteristics and character.

But Jesus is not just an outline of God. All the fullness of God dwells in him permanently with nothing missing (v. 19). This is Paul's counter argument to the Gnostic heresy of Jesus being one of many intermediaries.

Jesus is the Creator, Redeemer, Sustainer. He is the one through whom we and all of fallen creation can be reconciled to God. Since the Gnostics thought matter was evil, it would give them pause to think that creation would one day be restored to its original state.

Take a moment to look at the grand description in the passage again. Jesus is over all creation, by him and for him all things were created, he is before all things, all things hold together in him, all God's fullness dwells in him, through him God desires all things to be reconciled to him. Jesus is the initiator and the goal of creation as well as the one who holds everything together.

Paul goes further. He says Christ is the Church's head. This isn't in the sense of a figurehead, but of a physical head without which a body can't even live, let alone operate. He is the seat of the Church's right thinking and acting. Without him the Church is decapitated and as ineffective as a corpse.

Jesus is the Church's source and living Lord as well. By his resurrection, he is Lord over life and death. Oneness with Christ is the true sign of a Christian. We rejoice in him, our all in all.

Christ in You

'God wanted everyone, not just Jews, to know this rich and glorious secret inside and out, regardless of their background, regardless of their religious standing. The mystery in a nutshell is just this: Christ is in you, therefore you can look forward to sharing in God's glory. It's that simple. That is the substance of our Message' (v. 27, MSG).

Paul describes himself as an apostle of Christ (v.1), a servant of the gospel (v. 23) and by God's commission, a servant of the Church to whom he offers the Word of God (v. 25). His life's task is to offer everyone an open secret, the gospel of hope – salvation in Christ.

Paul willingly identifies with Christ and his Church, which includes suffering for Christ's sake so that the gospel can spread further. Paul intentionally calls it a mystery which has been disclosed to believers. The secret unfolds to those who come to Christ. Rather than being exclusive, it is inclusive. In Christ we are justified and Christ dwells in all his followers – even Gentiles.

The aim of Christ's reconciliation is our holiness (v. 22). No doubt the false teaching in Colosse spurred him to warn and teach everyone. Paul proclaims Christ for the purpose of presenting everyone whole in Christ (v. 28).

Jews might object that salvation was meant for the chosen people. Gnostics might say that salvation was intended for the intellectually elite. Paul says it is for everyone. How radical that must have seemed to people caught in advantaged or disadvantaged segments of cultures or religions!

Anyone who prepares, presents and applies the gospel message knows that teaching truth is hard work, whether in person or in print. Even though in prison, Paul acknowledges that it is God who empowers, energises and enables his non-stop labour for the gospel.

And it is God who continues to do the same for us. Praise him!

> God in you, God in me,
> Making us all we can be.
> Created in his image,
> Let us live in his will.
> God in you, God in me.
> *William Himes*

Hidden Treasure

'That they may know the mystery of God, namely, Christ, in whom are hidden all the treasures of wisdom and knowledge' (vv. 2, 3).

Paul spoke of suffering for Christ. Now he says he especially struggles inwardly for the Colossians and for other believers who don't know him personally yet for whom he is concerned. His struggles involve clarifying critical doctrines of faith – the incarnation and atonement. Since he is confined, he must struggle for them through letter and in prayer.

He prays that believers have courageous hearts and be interwoven in love. That unity leads to being equipped with critical, practical wisdom as well as wisdom of head and heart. Such a church can assess situations well, know the truth and communicate it. Where is this multifaceted wisdom found? It's hidden in Christ.

The Gnostics believed that the lofty knowledge needed for salvation was hidden from common view. They even named their books containing such knowledge 'hidden' because they were meant for the special few. By using the same Greek word for hidden, Paul confronts their heresy and says that for Christians, God's hidden wisdom in Christ is available to all.

A church that is equipped with the wisdom Paul espouses can resist even persuasive arguments of smooth talkers. Although unable to be with the Colossians, Paul says he is with them in spirit and is encouraged by how solidly disciplined they are and how firmly they hold their faith in Christ.

Such positive comments could inspire the wavering to hold on and set the tone for his appeal to them when Paul reminds them of their foundations. In what may also be a vote of confidence in their teacher, Epaphras, he counsels continuance in the Christian life as they were taught when they received Christ.

The Christian life is a walk of faith. It's a life of growth through commitment to the word and prayer. It's a way of continuous thanksgiving. Faith, growth and gratitude blend together and complement and develop each other in our lives.

To ponder:

A treasure of wisdom: a grateful attitude makes us more aware and responsive.

Beware of Add-ons

'For in Christ all the fulness of the Deity lives in bodily form,
and you have been given fulness in Christ, who is the Head over
every power and authority' (vv. 9, 10).

After advising believers to keep walking with Christ, Paul warns of the heresy that could disrupt that walk. Perhaps Colosse's location lent itself to mixing Judaism with Asian philosophy. Gnosticism developed extravagant systems of thought.

There may have been an attractive mystique about such unearthly ideas, but Paul saw their danger. He alerts believers to the deceptions of heretics: 'They spread their ideas through the empty traditions of human beings and the empty superstitions of spirit beings' (v. 8, *MSG*).

Whether through philosophy or astrology (v. 8), compulsory circumcision (v. 11), rules and observances (vv. 16, 20–23), or worship of angels (v. 18), the false teachers insist on adding their pet views as requisites to Christian belief. They don't hold Christ to be the unique revelation of God or sufficient in himself, so they devise elaborate additions.

Paul says that even the Old Testament systems were only previews of what God planned to reveal in Christ: 'These are a shadow of the things that were to come; the reality, however, is found in Christ' (v. 17). Resist those who would bring you into bondage. Watch out for the legalists, vain philosophers, those who would judge or give false or exclusive teaching.

Focus fully on Christ. The Christian life is all about him, about pleasing him and honouring him. When it comes to the truth of the gospel, add-ons or substitutes of solely human origin are suspect. Some religious rules may seem striking, but ultimately they are powerless. If we've decided to follow Jesus, we won't need to count on externals or making an impression.

Keep Christ central. He is our head. Our principles of living are based on him. We are complete in him. *The Message* says: 'You don't need a telescope, a microscope or a horoscope to realise the fullness of Christ, and the emptiness of the universe without him. When you come to him, that fullness comes together for you, too. His power extends over everything' (vv. 9, 10). Hallelujah!

Our Heart's Orientation

'For you died, and your life is now hidden with Christ in God' (v. 3).

Paul covered the Colossian church's controversy in the first two chapters; he now goes on to encourage right living and thinking. Christians died to sin and are raised with Christ, so should act and think that way. We seek to please Christ here and one day live with him in heaven. Christ is with God, so we who are in Christ should deliberately concentrate on the things of God and let them inform the choices we make and the way we live.

He isn't calling for asceticism or living by formalism or humanly devised rules to ensure divine acceptance. At the close of the previous chapter he denounced that. He is calling for living in this world by a power which transcends this world, the power of the risen Christ.

He isn't calling for a disdain of the physical things that God created. That would be Gnostic. But he is warning about lifting them out of their proper place or purpose. Temporal things need to serve eternal ones (2 Corinthians 4:18).

'Hidden with Christ in God' is a place of stability and safety as we shelter in the secret place of God (Psalm 91:1). The full implication of such a position won't become visible until Christ returns. Christ is our life now. And that will be apparent one day when we share in his glory. It will be the day of reversals when God's way will stand vindicated and victorious over all others.

That's why we set our minds on eternal things now. It takes intention and practice to see beyond the moment, to keep an eternal perspective. The Word and the Holy Spirit are our primary aides in setting our heart's focus on things above.

Even without overt declarations, we announce what we live for by the way we use our discretionary time and resources, our lives. Jesus said where our treasure is our hearts will be (Matthew 6:21). The cross is our point of reference.

Paul says Christ is our life (v. 4). In other letters he testifies: 'For to me, to live is Christ and to die is gain' (Philippians 1:21) and 'I have been crucified with Christ and I no longer live, but Christ lives in me. The life I live in the body, I live by faith in the Son of God, who loved me and gave himself for me' (Galatians 2:20). Amen.

On With the New

'Now you're dressed in a new wardrobe. Every item of your new way of life is custom-made by the Creator, with his label on it. All the old fashions are now obsolete' (v.10, MSG).

Paul expresses theology first, and then the ethical mandates that naturally follow. As in other letters, Paul emphasises that right living flows from a right relationship with Christ.

Paul's reminder to believers to cut off evil behaviours shows that an individual has a part to play in his new life in Christ. The Christian life is not automatic, but we move forward with intentional right living and decision-making in cooperation with the Holy Sprit.

In verses 5–9 Paul specifies certain sensual sins and behaviours that he's aware of in Colossian believers and that must end. *The Message* says they present 'a life shaped by things and feelings instead of by God'. In some way each of the sins identified is a form of idolatry and is evidence of dependence on gratifying desire rather than reliance on God. Perpetuating any of them jeopardises salvation (Ephesians 5:5).

Many houses built on hills in western Pennsylvania, USA, have an additional special entrance on the lower level at the back. Originally these accommodated coalminers or steelworkers in the family. When they returned from work covered with dust or grime, they could enter the house, strip off their work clothes and rinse down before putting on clean clothes and going upstairs.

Paul would have liked the analogy. He uses the image of stripping off old dirty clothes to address getting rid of particular social sins: nursed anger, rage, wickedness, slander, foul-mouthed talk and lying. He doesn't leave it there. He tells us what we should put on.

The attributes he lists deal with relationships: heartfelt compassion, active kindness, humility before God, gentleness with others, self-restraint in the face of provocation. He mentions several of these qualities in Ephesians 4:2. We recognise some from the fruit of the spirit in Galatians 5:22, 23.

The new self is a renewed self. It's not the old self gradually becoming new. It is the new self in Christ, becoming more and more like Jesus in the midst of the community of believers, the Church.

Forget-him-nots

While some countries celebrate a Sunday of thanksgiving today, we can all join with David in doxology for God's goodness to us.

> Praise the LORD, O my soul;
>   all my inmost being, praise his holy name.
> Praise the LORD, O my soul,
>   and forget not all his benefits –
> who forgives all your sins
>   and heals all your diseases,
> who redeems your life from the pit
>   and crowns you with love and compassion,
> who satisfies your desires with good things
>   so that your youth is renewed like the eagle's.
> The LORD works righteousness
>   and justice for all the oppressed.
> He made known his ways to Moses,
>   his deeds to the people of Israel:
> The LORD is compassionate and gracious,
>   slow to anger, abounding in love.
> He will not always accuse,
>   nor will he harbour his anger for ever;
> he does not treat us as our sins deserve
>   or repay us according to our iniquities.
> For as high as the heavens are above the earth,
>   so great is his love for those who fear him;
> as far as the east is from the west,
>   so far has he removed our transgressions from us.
> As a father has compassion on his children,
>   so the LORD has compassion on those who fear him.

Wear an Obi

'Put on the new self, which is being renewed in knowledge in the image of its Creator' (v. 10).

Paul states that the new self is being transformed in the Creator's image. In Colossians 1 Paul said all things were created by and for Christ. So we can say that Christians, his new creation, are being renewed in the image of Christ as they yield to his Holy Spirit's promptings. In Ephesians, Paul says it this way: 'Put on the new self, created to be like God in true righteousness and holiness' (Ephesians 4:24).

In verse 11 Paul counters current thinking of exclusivity. In Christ, racial, ritual, cultural, linguistic, social, economic, national or religious barriers come down. Nothing keeps a person from salvation except sin. The ancient world imposed many barriers. First-century believers were products of their society's prejudices. Even today we need to think about our own natural biases and remember that 'Christ is all and is in all' (v. 11).

In verse 12 Paul addresses his Gentile readers as God's chosen, holy and beloved people. These words originally described the Jewish people. At every opportunity Paul shows how wide the circle of God's love really is.

Besides wearing the new wardrobe of grace, Paul tells us to forgive one another. He implies that in doing so for others, we benefit ourselves as well. The standard is forgiving others as the Lord forgives us. Paul echoes what Jesus said about forgiveness (Matthew 6, 18; Luke 6, 7, 17).

Over everything, wear the one thing that makes all the traits of the Christian hold together: love.

Imagine carefully putting on the multilayered kimono. The final essential part is the *obi*. It's a yards-long piece of exquisite silk which winds around the kimono at the waist. When an expert ties it into a bow at the back, it looks perfect, as if preformed. Even if it is plainer than the colourful kimono, it is beautiful in form.

The *obi's* function of holding everything together and being the finishing touch seems an apt analogy for 'and over all these virtues put on love, which binds them all together in perfect unity' (v. 14).

Sing and Keep Going

'Let the word of Christ dwell in you richly as you teach and admonish one another with all wisdom, and as you sing psalms, hymns and spiritual songs with gratitude in your hearts to God' (v. 16).

A few verses earlier Paul called the Colossians to exercise Christ-like attitudes in their dealings with each other. He must be writing in response to reports of serious conflicts. He continues by urging that, instead of worrying about getting their own way, believers should turn arbitrations over to God. If Christ's peace is the umpire or arbiter in each Christian, it will be more likely to be so between the members of his body as well.

If we all listen to the direction of our divine conductor, we'll more readily be brought in tune and harmony with each other. The closer we are to Christ, the closer we come to each other. Paul adds that Christians are to be thankful people. A grateful mindset is the partner of a peaceful heart.

If our lives not only welcome the Word of Christ but also provide it with a place to live, we'll act by its precepts more and more reflexively. Only from such a solid basis can we counsel and teach one another in the Church. In Colossians 1 Paul said he and other leaders did just that for the sake of presenting everyone perfect in Christ. Now he passes the responsibility to the whole body of believers.

If from a position of God's Word Christians, in tune with the Spirit, counsel and teach with wisdom and sing with grateful hearts, God will be glorified. *The Message* concludes verse 16 with: 'And sing, sing your hearts out to God!'

We have so many types of songs today. Psalms and portions of Epistles may have been what the earliest Christians sang for worship, mutual edification and encouragement. No doubt they did so even when they met secretly. We sing for the same reasons: 'We sing the ancient song of creation to its Creator, we sing the new song of the redeemed to their Redeemer.'[9]

Singing doesn't seem to be optional, relegated to the few or restricted to times of public worship. There's a song in the heart of every believer.

Whatever

'And whatever you do, whether in word or deed, do it all in the name of the Lord Jesus, giving thanks to God the Father through him' (v. 17).

There's a linden-wood sculpture appliquéd to cherry-wood panels on the wall of the Claremont Lobby at the Interchurch Centre in New York City. Artist Adlai Hardin created a tree with a family as its base and people busy in nineteen occupations as its branches. The work includes the words it illustrates: 'Whatever you do, do all to the glory of God' (1 Corinthians 10:31, *NASB*).

The sculpture could just as well illustrate Colossians 3:17 and 3:23. After Paul tells us to let the Word be central to our teaching and singing, he says whatever we do, whether through words or actions, we should do it in the name of Jesus. Then he applies that general principle within the family, at the workplace and in relationships.

Whatever we do in our daily lives should be done in Jesus' name. We can take that to mean for his sake or as if done for him. When Jesus spoke of future judgment he said, 'I tell you the truth, whatever you did for one of the least of these brothers of mine, you did for me' (Matthew 25:40).

We can also think of living in Jesus' name as living with his authority as his ambassadors. Or we can think of it as we do the concept of praying in Jesus' name which means in agreement with God's will and to glorify Jesus. What matters is the essential spirit of and purpose behind the prayer, not words tacked on as a formula for success. So too with whatever we do.

The scope seems so broad, but Paul's injunction includes anything we do in word or action. Besides what we do routinely or vocationally, it means taking stock of our leisure time, our conversations, our choices, our interactions with people in public and private.

If we act in dependence on the Spirit of Christ, there will be plenty of reasons to give God thanks. For the third time in three verses Paul urges thanksgiving.

When we live for the Lord first in everything, we give first-rate service to those for whom we work and we treat those for whom we are responsible fairly (vv. 23, 24; 4:1).

———

To ponder:

How can I live and work more and more fully in Jesus' name?

Unlimited Resources

*'Be earnest and unwearied in prayer, being on the alert in it
and in your giving of thanks' (v. 2, WNT).*

Thanksgiving must be important. Paul mentions it frequently. He might tell us that it is a means of grace. In verse 2 Paul says it should be part of our prayer commitment. He couples being thankful with being watchful. If we have a grateful attitude, we tend to be alert to what's happening around us which in turn gives us more reasons to be thankful.

Earlier Paul told the Colossians that he prays for them (1:3–12). Now he requests prayer for himself. He doesn't ask the Colossians to pray for his release from prison or for his comfort. He doesn't ask for prayer to be relieved of his assignment. He asks for prayer for more opportunities to tell more people about Christ more clearly. He wants hindrances to that mission minimised. He wants the power to persevere.

We know, as Paul did, that Satan's obstacles can be thwarted only through prayer. That was especially clear to Paul because of the limitations of prison. Sometimes our own limitations of health, resources or abilities bring us to the same conclusion. Instead of resignation to only having prayer as recourse, we should be glad that we've exhausted our self-sufficient means. God is not limited!

> He giveth more grace as our burdens grow greater,
> He sendeth more strength as our labours increase,
> To added afflictions he addeth his mercy,
> To multiplied trials he multiplies peace.
>
> When we have exhausted our store of endurance,
> When our strength has failed ere the day is half done,
> When we reach the end of our hoarded resources
> Our Father's full giving is only begun.
>
> His love has no limits, his grace has no measure,
> His power no boundary known unto men;
> For out of his infinite riches in Jesus
> He giveth, and giveth, and giveth again.
> *Annie Johnson Flint*

Disarming Faith

'Be wise in the way you act toward outsiders; make the most of every opportunity' (v. 5).

In addition to the efficacy of prayer, Paul reminds the Colossians again about the power of Christian example among non-Christians. Let them see wise, tactful behaviour. Show Christ-like living at every opportunity.

In 2006 a gunman killed five children and critically injured five others at a one-room Amish school in Pennsylvania, USA. On the day of the shooting a grandfather of one of the girls warned some young people not to hate the killer, who had also killed himself.

Amish members offered comfort and forgiveness to the killer's family. His widow replied: 'Your love for our family has helped to provide the healing we so desperately need. Your compassion has reached beyond our family, beyond our community, and is changing our world, and for this we sincerely thank you.'

Some people criticised the sweeping acts of forgiveness while others were supportive. The world was in awe of the Amish response to tragedy. They demonstrated their faith in extreme circumstances.

In addition to acting judiciously, Paul says Christians should speak graciously. Conversations should be seasoned or prepared with salt. This is the only place Paul uses the metaphor. In ancient Greece and Rome, salt in speech referred to its wittiness and pungency.

In Ephesians 4:29 Paul expands on appropriate communication: 'Do not let any unwholesome talk come out of your mouths, but only what is helpful for building others up according to their needs, that it may benefit those who listen.'

While pleasing speech is desirable, it needn't be bland. Charming, witty speech is not unchristian. Salt makes food palatable, it penetrates and is pure. Our speech should make dialogue enriching while remaining truthful and honest. Even its tenor should stimulate interest in what makes us perpetually hopeful (1 Peter 3:15).

Finish with Grace

'Grace be with you' (v. 18).

When writers, directors or actors are honoured they give acceptance speeches. Typically the recipients start by thanking an endless list of people, often including people behind the scenes who enabled their success. Unlike their professional work, the speeches are often forgettable. But those who are named in them find them memorable.

Paul doesn't directly thank his colleagues, but sends greetings from several who are with him, people who have dared to be associated with him in prison. He names them.

First he commends the messengers who carry the letter to Colosse for him, Tychicus and Onesimus. These faithful believers would verbally fill in more personal details about the situation in Rome. Tychicus is Paul's trusted envoy who carried other letters for Paul. Onesimus is a runaway slave going back home to Colosse, but the apostle refers to him as a brother. Imagine his testimony!

Next Paul mentions fellow Jewish Christians Aristarchus, Mark and Jesus called Justus. In verse 11 Paul says they are the only Jewish believers who have been his supporters in prison. Mark is the one who quit Paul's earlier missionary team, but here Paul just says he's the cousin of Barnabas and commends him. Mark's restoration implies his change of heart and Paul's accepting approval of him.

Paul names the three Gentile believers who are with him. Epaphras is the Colossians' prayer warrior. He knows their needs personally and cares deeply about their growth in the Lord. Even while away from them he works hard for believers of all three area churches, perhaps as their overseer or circuit pastor.

Paul calls Luke a dear friend and doctor. He stayed with Paul to the end (2 Timothy 4:11). It is interesting that two of the Gospel-writers, Mark and Luke, are with Paul in Rome. They could give him accurate information about Jesus' ministry. Finally Paul merely names Demas, nothing more. Perhaps Paul already wondered about his commitment (2 Timothy 4:10). For now, Demas is present.

Paul signs his name, asks that readers remember his chains, his credentials, and closes with what he knows is enough for all: grace.

Anticipation

'The Mighty One has done great things for me – holy is his name' (v. 49).

On the Sunday closest to St Andrew's Day, 30 November, Advent begins. We move deliberately toward what we know comes soon, Christmas. Today we think of the encounter of Mary and Elizabeth. They shared their anticipation of Christ's coming in a singular way that informs our preparation.

Elizabeth's Blessing (based on Luke 1:39–45)

They met as sisters in a common bond of pregnancy
one too young – O the scandal!
the other too old – O the surprise
after decades of bitter barrenness and shame.

Each bowed in blessing before the other
and their babies bowed too.
One the forerunner
who would announce the coming of the Saviour
the other the Saviour
coming for his forerunner
and for all like him
each baby the living proof
that God delights to do the impossible.

In this mellow season of my life
may I be like Elizabeth
passing on blessing
to the Marys who come after me
helping to midwife their dreams
at the same time
delighting in the stirrings
that signal a surprising new birth
taking shape within myself.

Barbara Sampson

Praying Towards a Happy Christmas

(An Advent series by guest writer Major Rachel Tickner)

Rachel Tickner is a Salvation Army officer whose service has been focused on social work and training, in the United Kingdom, Kenya and Uganda. She has served most recently as Social Services Secretary and Director of Training for the Uganda Command. Her experiences are reflected in some of the readings. She writes:

Each year we anticipate Christmas. The excitement gathers as we approach the holy day. In the prophecies of Isaiah we hear that anticipation, but it is very different from ours for we have the benefit of hindsight. We know that the Christ was born. Most of us know the nativity story well and have celebrated it year after year after year.

As we look forward to Christmas we may be thinking of shopping or carolling, of presents or cooking. We may remember previous Christmases filled with joy or tainted with sorrows of events personal to us.

Leading up to Christmas we will share verses from Isaiah and use them to stimulate our prayers as we prepare to celebrate the birth of Christ.

Listen

'Hear, O heavens! Listen, O earth! For the LORD has spoken: "I reared children and brought them up, but they have rebelled against me"' (v. 2).

The Lord is sad when he speaks these words. Our heavenly Father had troublesome children then and has troublesome children today. Those Christians who have tried and failed to rear God-fearing families wonder where they went wrong. God understands the anxious parent.

'Hear' and 'Listen' are commands. Sound is very important. We may like to speak or sing, but hearing certain sounds stirs the heart as nothing else. Imagine hearing the angel chorus announce the birth of Jesus. If that is too difficult, then remember how you tingled on hearing some special music. Handel's 'Hallelujah Chorus' is a favourite for many people; a variety of choirs and bands and soloists can touch the soul; though not all sounds have a happy effect: the toddler's drum, the parents' argument, the neighbour's music – sometimes the chords they touch are unpleasant ones.

And how is it that imperfect music shared out of a full heart can still touch the soul? A boy attended a week-long music school. He received little love at home and did not enjoy school. He had received no music lessons but was naturally musical. He was asked to sing a solo and although he breathed in the wrong places and dropped all his 'H's there was not a dry eye in the room, because in his singing there was something very beautiful.

On another occasion a young man who was a candidate for the ministry stood up to preach. He had a stammer and the congregation leant forward and willed him on in silent encouragement. Listening can be a positive, loving act.

When we have a choice, what will we listen to this Advent season – favourite music, readings? Will we make time for silence? Perhaps our truest worship should be listening prayers, not speaking ones, for when God speaks to us it is wise to listen.

Let's Party!

' *"Your New Moon festivals and your appointed feasts my soul hates. They have become a burden to me; I am weary of bearing them"* ' *(v. 14)*.

At this time of year we fill our time with parties, concerts, carol services, feasts, shopping sprees and pantomimes because we enjoy them, though sometimes they become pressures. Our feet ache, and the shops, for all their multitudinous displays, sometimes fail to provide the right present for a special uncle.

What should be a wonderful meal is blighted for the host because the recipe or the cooker or the clock is not cooperating. The special carol service is planned to the last detail but for one reason or another someone is disappointed.

The giving and receiving of pleasure should not have to be hard work. We have different temperaments. Those with spontaneous personalities may need to give the gift of consideration for their more planning-oriented friends and the planners may need to be willing to give the gift of relaxing their expectations – all in the spirit of love.

We should heed God's words to the Israelites. He was fed up with their festivals and feasts. There were even too many sacrifices – though the problem was surely the spirit in which they were offered. 'I have more than enough of burnt offerings,' God declared (v. 11). I wonder, does he cringe at some of our Christmas celebrations? Should we think twice about some of the things we do at this season of the year, or at least the spirit in which we do them?

Nevertheless, if our celebrations bring joy, God will be happy that we are enjoying celebrating the birth of his Son. He gave us gifts of hospitality, generosity, music, time, family. He gave us joy itself.

Christina Rosetti concludes her poem, 'Love came down at Christmas' with:

> Love shall be our token,
> Love be yours and love be mine,
> Love to God and all men,
> Love for plea and gift and sign.

Since joy and love came down at Christmas, let's prepare now to celebrate and to share God's love with others. How can that be a burden?

Widows and Orphans

'Your rulers are rebels, companions of thieves, they all love bribes and chase after gifts. They do not defend the cause of the fatherless; the widow's case does not come before them' (v. 23).

God was angry with the Israelites, for a reason all too familiar to many of us. There seems never to have been a time when our world has been without a dictator ruling cruelly somewhere, and today is no exception. Bribery and corruption still make life difficult for widows and orphans and low-income families struggling to make an honest living. Situations in the daily news should call us to pray.

Many countries have Christian communities who find it difficult to live according to their faith in a country governed in a culture of corruption. They need ministry and teaching in the style of the apostle Paul's letters. Others are being salt in their communities and are really making a difference: they are defending the fatherless and the widows.

'Coffee Coffee' is a Ugandan orphan, so-called because he sold coffee in the market. He lived with his grandfather but received little food or warmth and no education. He ran away to Kampala. He was taken to a Salvation Army officer, who placed him in the care of a Salvationist, a poorly paid gardener who looked after him for several weeks, sharing what little he had before the lad returned home.

His old friends and neighbours were delighted to see Coffee Coffee again and when they saw how well The Salvation Army had looked after him, they encouraged The Salvation Army to find him a permanent place in their Tororo children's home, with a Norwegian Christian paying toward his daily upkeep and a Christian group in Canada providing further support.

This Christmas, let's remember Coffee Coffee – now called Tony – and all similar children around the world who need the protection of those who see it as their God-given charge to care for widows and orphans. We can pray and we can give.

To ponder:

'Religion that God our Father accepts as pure and faultless is this: to look after orphans and widows in their distress and to keep oneself from being polluted by the world.'

(James 1:27)

Light

'Come, O house of Jacob, let us walk in the light of the LORD' (v. 5).

Christmas is a time for lights: lights on the Christmas tree, lights in the windows, lights to encourage Christmas shoppers. In the purest sense these are a symbol of Jesus, the Light of the World. Many churches have beautiful stained glass windows and you can gaze in awe at the scenes and the colours as the light shines through them.

Learning from some nursery-school teachers, I discovered that it's quite simple to mix poster paints with washing-up liquid and paint directly onto a window – with a damp cloth in hand to erase mistakes. Since the discovery of this skill it's been my delight to paint many windows at Christmas. The lamb is copied from one Christmas card and the wise men from another, and sometimes there is a little creativity as well.

I most enjoyed painting the windows of The Salvation Army's Hopetown hostel for women in the East End of London. At that time the centre had plate-glass double doors, with additional glass side panels. The nativity scene was painted across the four panels and I carefully ensured that no figure would be cut in two when the doors swung open. Every homeless woman entered the hostel through the stable doors and the message it gave was that a welcome awaited each one, just as Jesus waits to welcome each one of us in prayer today.

Doors that are in constant use can get damaged. During the weeks of Advent, the animal paintings would get scuffed and faces scratched, so there would be running repairs with a paintbrush. But at night the light in reception shone through the doors, telling the Christmas story. None of the sophisticated lights in the West End of London, with its shops and theatres, had quite the same impact. Even with its scratches, the nativity scene on the doors of Hopetown hostel welcomed each woman into a new life.

> Open wide the stable door,
> Monarchs rich and shepherds poor
> Wait to tread the holy floor
> Where lies the Son of God.
> *Arch R. Wiggins*[10]

Trust in God

'Stop trusting in man, who has but a breath in his nostrils.
Of what account is he?' (v. 22)

Coming down the stairs on Christmas morning at the age of seven, I recognised the smell of Christmas: a mixture of vegetables and stuffing, talcum powder, new wood and oranges. My young brain remembered the smells from previous years and I was excited. In adult life the aromas are different, but still turkey and stuffing, mince pies and, yes, Brussels sprouts seem to breathe Christmas.

These are very different from the smells of new baby, animals and straw of the first Christmas, and later the rich perfumes of the magi. All give Christmas a special dimension. When we have a nativity play with real animals it is very different from having a toy lamb!

We are human beings, and simple ones at that. The nose which enjoys the scent of Christmas is the same nose which breathes in the breath of life. The prophet says we are just that, a breath in the nostrils. Even our respected leaders are but a breath in their nostrils as well. Of what account are they? We should trust in God, and in his son, the Messiah, even though 'he was despised and rejected by men, a man of sorrows, and familiar with suffering' (Isaiah 53:3).

As we capture the transient whiff of Christmas we are filled with anticipation. Surely it is possible to transcend this temporal joy and realise the glory which is complete confidence in God.

Reginald Heber wrote in his carol 'Brightest and best':

> Say, shall we yield him, in costly devotion,
> Odours of Edom, and off'rings divine,
> Gems of the mountain and pearls of the ocean,
> Myrrh from the forest or gold from the mine?
>
> Vainly we offer each ample oblation;
> Vainly with gifts would his favour secure;
> Richer by far is the heart's adoration;
> Dearer to God are the pray'rs of the poor.

Night and Day

'Then the LORD will create . . . a cloud of smoke by day and a glow
of flaming fire by night; over all the glory will be a canopy. It will
be a shelter and shade from the heat of the day, and a refuge and
hiding-place from the storm and rain' (vv. 5, 6).

This reading will have reminded the Israelites of God's protection when he led them out of bondage (Exodus 13:21). God protects us in different ways at different times. Some people are plagued at night by fears: the mind will not rest and troubles seem huge. For others it's the day which has pressures and there is solace and rest at night.

At one time I worked on the Midnight Patrol in London. During the day those in difficulty could blend into the crowd. At night they were more obvious. Those who usually did not pray might well cry out, in their distress, 'O God!', and God would hear them. Paul was one such lad. Having found a bed for him at a hostel, I and my companion were walking down to the underground to see him onto the last train.

In spite of his call of distress, Paul told us he didn't believe in God. We could only say, 'But it makes you think, doesn't it? You had nowhere to go and didn't know what to do. Now you're on the way to a hostel.' Then his train came and off he went. We knew he would wake up in the morning in a centre where prayers would be said. Our prayers went with him. God cared and was providing the protection he needed.

As well as my memory of that young lad, I have a vivid picture in my mind of visiting a refugee camp on the Uganda–Kenya border at a time of trouble. There was no shelter from the relentless sun. We returned to our vehicle and found three toddlers sitting underneath it in the shadow it offered.

The God who gives shade to the youngest refugees and shelter to young men lost in a big city provides loving protection for us as well.

> As the bird beneath her feathers
> Guards the objects of her care,
> So the Lord his children gathers,
> Spreads his wings, and hides us there.
> *Thomas Kelly*

Gift-Giving Season

'Thanks be to God for his indescribable gift!' (v. 15).

It's St Nicholas Day. In some countries it's a day for gift-giving in the spirit and memory of a kind, generous Christian leader. In the fourth century, Nicholas was Bishop of Myra in what is now Turkey. I have known some of his modern counterparts.

One with minimal resources, who lived in government housing, delighted in giving whatever she had – including allowing the children of neighbours to make her tiny garden their own. Another senior citizen who attended our women's meetings lived frugally. No one knew she had amassed wealth until her will was read and people who had shown her kindness even decades before received sizeable cheques.

There are people who shower us with daily prayer year after year. Some correspond with people living far from their homeland. Others give to encourage believers whom they've never met. Prompted by love, they're in a vast league of anonymous givers like Nicholas. But even more, generous Christians are reflections of a bountiful God, the source of all good gifts (James 1:17). We celebrate God's best gift, Jesus, especially as we approach another Christmas.

One Christmas More

The star draws near again
to ancient Bethlehem.
And still we seek,
though famished, weak,
to catch a glimpse of him
who gives one Christmas more
from time's depleting store.
He calls us down the dwindling year:
'Come and dine, your life is here.'
Here in the lowly shed
where dogs and cattle are fed
is the best, the living Bread
fragrant on the hearth.

Marlene Chase

Hurt

*'What more could have been done for my vineyard than
I have done for it?' (v. 4)*

This song of the vineyard reveals God the gardener. God is hurt: he has done everything he can in the vineyard, but still the reward is bad fruit. God looks for justice and righteousness in his people but sees bloodshed and hears cries of distress (v. 7). Jesus uses this same allegory in Matthew 21:33–41.

Christmas is a family time, and because of our ideals we are more vulnerable at Christmas. We miss those who have died and also mourn those who have turned their back on the family home. God offers redemption through Jesus. The Christmas Baby was the catalyst to bring good fruit into the garden. Jesus said: 'I am the true vine, and my Father is the gardener' (John 15:1).

At this time of year we are preparing to welcome the Baby who brings unity and goodness and a direct path to God. As we do so we need to be at one with God, our families, our neighbours and our world in order to welcome the Christ-child. This is not easy. God was hurt by the Israelites. He is hurt today by the anguish we cause him. But he is still ready to welcome us and restore us.

Because Christmas has become such a secular event for so many people, it gives Christians opportunity for simple, non-threatening overtures. Christmas baking, Christmas cards, Christmas presents can all be shared. These simple actions can break down barriers and end estrangements within families, isolation within communities and insecurities between individuals who lack the confidence to make contact. The first step is always prayer.

To pray:

Lord, help me to be an instrument of comfort and encouragement for someone who is hurting as I delight someone with your love this Christmas time.

To ponder:

God doesn't want us to remember things he is willing to forget.

Balance

'*But the* LORD *Almighty will be exalted by his justice, and the holy God will show himself holy by his righteousness. Then sheep will graze as in their own pasture; lambs will feed among the ruins of the rich*' (*vv. 16, 17*).

There are lots of 'woes' in this passage: woe to those who 'add house to house', to those who drink, to the deceitful. The 'brawlers and revellers' are sadly relevant to the Christmas season. We live in a secular world. It is hard not to covet what our neighbour has, or what is shown so attractively on television.

The two short verses quoted above are the only rays of light set among the warnings of this reading. We serve a supremely just and holy God. This is good to hold on to.

Memories of happy Christmases in the past when we, or our parents, had so little may help us get our priorities right in the way we celebrate, but might not help youngsters cope with the peer-pressures from their friends. We don't have to be martyrs and go without everything, or make our children do so, in order to identify with those who have little; but we need to keep things in proportion if our celebrations are to be meaningful.

Nairobi is a city both of rich hotels and happy tourists, and of extreme poverty. A friend and I made up a number of Christmas food parcels. To the basics of maize flour, rice, beans and oil we added treats of jam, biscuits and soap – and a little money for meat. We asked our church minister to deliver the parcels to needy families.

One particular woman was not at home any of the times the pastor visited. She had been in hospital and travelled home with borrowed bus fare on Christmas Eve. She worried about finding the means to feed her children. The pastor tried once more and found her at home. The woman wept with joy and praised God when she received the parcel. For her, Scripture had come true: 'Lambs will feed among the ruins of the rich' (v. 17).

To ponder:

Is the Lord prompting us to 'feed my lambs' this Advent?

Calling

'Then I heard the voice of the LORD saying, "Whom shall I send? And who will go for us?" And I said, "Here am I. Send me!"' (v. 8)

The art teacher read the first three verses of this chapter to her class. 'Now paint what you have heard,' she said. Many groans were heard as the children tried to paint seraphs with six wings: two for flying, two to cover the face and two to cover the feet. The attempts were crude. The teacher pinned every picture on the wall. There was a mass of yellow and orange paint. A powerful heavenly host looked down on the classroom. No child would forget that art room, or the Scripture. Without preaching, this woman helped children to experience the contents of the Bible.

Isaiah saw a mighty host of angels. One took a live coal and touched Isaiah's mouth. Isaiah was an unworthy man of unclean lips, of a people of unclean lips. Yet God chose Isaiah and equipped him for his task. God has a purpose and call for each of us. God wants some to be preachers, some teachers, some medics. But it would be a terrible world if we had no plumbers. Each of us has a part to play. We should remember, too, that our calling might not be in our employment but in our living. God calls us to be 'salt' in our community.

How does God call? How do I know I am called? God speaks to us personally and speaks in different ways. If you feel a tingling sensation when you read 'Whom shall I send? And who will go for us?' then God is speaking to you. Some actually hear his voice, while others hear him speak through the words of others. Some are convicted because of situations, others have visions. God can use art or music or angels.

When there is uncertainty about calling we should ask God to speak clearly to us. He may get our attention through our senses to communicate a call to our hearts. We have his Word and his Spirit to help us clarify that a call is in line with his will.

Here am I, my Lord, send me,
I surrender all to obey thy call,
Here am I, my Lord, send me,
W. Walker (SASB 482)

Standing Firm

'If you do not stand firm in your faith, you will not stand at all' (v. 9).

This is the time of year for carolling. Children singing from door to door, big gala carol concerts and a Salvation Army band in the street or shopping centre. For someone blowing a brass instrument the first hour is good: the harmonies bring joy, people passing begin to walk in time with the music, and the spirit of Christmas is evident.

After the first hour, the harmonies are still good, the shoppers are still cheered, but the players are aware of a red nose, a crick in the back and feet beginning to numb. The rhythms encourage the band to wriggle their toes, the collectors come with requests from shoppers who want to hear their favourites – and sometimes additional blessing comes through a café, shop or office sending out a hot drink to warm the carollers.

As the band plays, shoppers are reminded of the Christmas message and many will be familiar with the words of the carols. The collectors often have opportunity to share the concerns of those listening. The little group (unless blessed by the hospitality of the big indoor shopping mall) gets colder and colder – but continues to give out the message.

Having done this one Saturday they continue through Advent, reminding people of the Christmas message. Many will also play in old people's homes and hospitals; some are committed to evenings as well as weekends – and they still need to do their Christmas shopping and preparations as well. Yet despite the irritations of cold weather and aches they return the next Saturday and indeed the next Christmas and the Christmas after that. Though literally standing, it is their faith that strengthens them and enables them to carol year after year after year – reminding us of today's key verse: 'If you do not stand firm in your faith, you will not stand at all.'

It's not just the Salvation Army band; many people put themselves out to make Christmas special for others. Thank God for them all this Advent season.

God With Us

'Therefore the Lord himself will give you a sign: The virgin will be with child and will give birth to a son, and will call him Immanuel' (v. 14).

Now at last we have a sign, a prophecy of the Christ-child. Isaiah is prophesying to Ahaz, king of Judah, who has just been defeated in battle. The prophesy comes more than 700 years before the birth of Christ, and is quoted within the birth narrative found in Matthew 1:18–25: 'All this took place to fulfil what the Lord had said through the prophet: "The virgin will be with child and will give birth to a son, and they will call him Immanuel" – which means, "God with us".'

Both Isaiah and Ahaz understood this prophecy to relate to the son of Ahaz and that it means he would bring salvation to the believers and save Judah. We don't always understand God.

When God sent his only Son he did something far more magnificent: Jesus truly was, and is, God with us. And he came for each one of us, not just one favoured tribe.

The eight verses of the now well-known thirteenth-century Latin antiphon, *'Veni, veni Emanuel'*, translated into English by John Mason Neale, both petitions God to come for his people and confirms that he indeed will come. We pray too:

> O come, O come, Immanuel,
> And ransom captive Israel,
> That mourns in lonely exile here
> Until the Son of God appear.
>
> O come, thou Day-spring, come and cheer
> Our spirits by thine advent here;
> Disperse the gloomy clouds of night,
> And death's dark shadows put to flight.
>
> O come, desire of nations, bind
> In one the hearts of all mankind;
> Bid thou our sad divisions cease,
> And be thyself our King of Peace.
>
> Rejoice, rejoice! Immanuel shall come to thee, O Israel.

God Is With Us

'Devise your strategy, but it will be thwarted; propose your plan,
but it will not stand, for God is with us' (v. 10).

There are still battles and warnings in this passage. A reference to Immanuel in verse 8 and the affirmation 'God is with us' in verse 10 emphasise our ever-present God. We are reminded that our plans are worthless without God. Sometimes we forget and race ahead, thinking we know what is needed and how it should be done. Then we are hurt and feel misunderstood when things go wrong, and we wonder why. We need to involve God in our planning, and we need always to trust him. We need wise counsel and most of all we need to pray.

Paul has great advice in Romans 8:28–39 for those who would be 'more than conquerors'. The passage gives strength for today. It includes some well known phrases: 'We know that in all things God works for the good of those who love him' (v. 28); 'If God is for us, who can be against us?' (v. 31); 'Neither height nor depth, nor anything else in all creation, will be able to separate us from the love of God that is in Christ Jesus our Lord' (v. 39).

'God with us' (Immanuel) is a stated fact. When we say, as today's text does, 'God *is* with us' we add the dimension of personal declaration and affirmation of that fact. We echo the spirit of Paul's verses in Romans.

Ahaz and his people did not directly know God; he spoke to them through Isaiah. This distant God was explained as someone they should fear when they disobeyed him. Now that we have Jesus we have a direct link with God. We have the possibility of being in personal relationship with him. If we are in relationship with him we can know his love and forgiveness each time we come to him.

To ponder:

How can I declare my testimony of God's goodness and grace to someone this Advent? God is with me.

The Promise

*'A shoot will come up from the stump of Jesse; from his roots
a Branch will bear fruit' (v. 1).*

The Promise whispered through the years
Moves ineluctably towards the appointed time.
The Word – dynamic verb
Fused and primed in eternity
Waits cradled in natal womb.
Heaven on tip-toe anticipates,
Satan shudders, divine threat realised.
Root and Rod are incarnate,
The Bruised Seed is planted.
Angel Choirs sing triumph's song
While Mary croons her lullaby:
His name will be Jesus!

Cliff Hurcum

Come, thou long-expected Jesus,
Born to set thy people free;
From our fears and sins release us,
Let us find our rest in thee.

All thy people's consolation,
Hope of all the earth thou art;
Dear desire of every nation,
Joy of every longing heart.

Born thy people to deliver,
Born a child and yet a King,
Born to reign in us for ever,
Now thy gracious Kingdom bring.

By thine own eternal Spirit
Rule in all our hearts alone;
By thine all-sufficient merit
Raise us to thy glorious throne.

Charles Wesley

Wise Men

*'When men tell you to consult mediums and spiritists, who whisper
and mutter, should not a people enquire of their God? Why consult
the dead on behalf of the living?' (v. 19)*

The Magi are biblical figures found in every nativity play. Those wise men who
came to worship the infant Jesus studied the stars and understood that the
'King of the Jews' had been born (Matthew 2:1–12). What could be wrong with
studying the stars for guidance – astrology? After all, God created the stars.

Horoscopes claim to be based on the stars and their positions in the sky when
we were born. Should Christians pay any attention to them? Some prophets
foretold the future, so people might ask what's the difference between them and
anyone who reads our palm or looks into a glass ball. Isn't it the source and
purpose of the knowledge?

Today's verse, echoing God's words in Leviticus 19:31, warns about mediums
and spiritists. Are we strong enough or wise enough to withstand evil we do not
understand or that is dressed up as harmless, popular culture? Don't we need a
standard against which to measure?

What is the purpose of considering such foretelling? Is it for our own
gratification or to truly know the will of our loving God? Recently a colleague
shared a dream. Neither he nor I understood it. We prayed and asked that if God
wanted to say something through this dream, he would reveal it through one of
his servants.

Questions may help us consider things we do not understand. The most
practical help is found in 1 John 4:1–6 where we find advice in testing the spirits:
the key is whether they acknowledge Jesus or not. The birth of Christ opened the
way for us to have power and wisdom to discern the good. If we cannot test
something with his name, then we cannot know that it is good. It's better that we
speak to God; and the Spirit of Truth will help us as we study God's Word.

> Jesus, the name high over all,
> In hell or earth or sky;
> Angels and men before him fall,
> And devils fear and fly.
>
> *Charles Wesley*

Walking in Darkness

'The people walking in darkness have seen a great light; on those living in the land of the shadow of death a light has dawned' (v. 2).

Some of our readings from Isaiah have displayed the depressing state of God's people straying far from him. But now we have the dawning of a great light.

Walking in the dark is very dangerous. In Uganda very few areas have working street lights. Car headlights find it hard to recognise anything that could indicate the edge or the centre of the road. Potholes do not always show up shadows. The nervous driver thinks there is a person on the edge of the road and then realises it is a tree. Or a driver narrowly misses a cyclist and then sees there's a jogger who isn't wearing reflective or white clothing. In the darkness, even the pedestrian risks tripping over a loose stone, falling into an uncovered manhole or being hit by a car.

In the dark our senses are heightened. The contrast of light is greater. We see stars which are not evident when we are among the bright lights of the city. In a power-cut, the light of a single match reveals the candle. The room lit by that single candle may be seen from a great distance. During the Second World War there were strict regulations about 'black-out' because the weakest light in the night could be strong enough to disclose a city's location to enemy aircraft.

This passage heralding the birth of Christ starts in the darkness with a glimmer of light. With the coming Messiah 'there will be no more gloom for those who were in distress' (v. 1). Isaiah goes on to point to the coming light. Then he pulls back the curtain and lets the brightness of the full prophecy burst on those walking in darkness. As hymnwriter William Hewley puts it:

> A light came out of darkness;
> No light, no hope had we,
> Till Jesus came from heaven
> Our light and hope to be.
> Oh, as I read the story
> From birth to dying cry,
> A longing fills my bosom
> To meet him by and by.

Name

'For to us a child is born, to us a son is given, and the government
will be on his shoulders, and he will be called Wonderful Counsellor,
Mighty God, Everlasting Father, Prince of Peace' (v. 6).

Some Christmas babies are especially named for this season with names such as Holly, Carol, Noel, Emmanuel, Gabrielle, Natalie (Christmas), Angela (messenger) and Tiffany (Epiphany). Other names or their variations reflect the qualities we hope for the child – Grace, Hope, Ernest.

Some choose names for other special reasons – to honour a relative, remember a notable film star or football hero, or entirely for their meaning: Beatrice (woman who blesses), Christine (belonging to Christ), Christopher (bearing Christ), Evangeline (of the gospel), John (Jehovah has been gracious), Theodore (gift of God).

In Isaiah we are promised Immanuel, Wonderful Counsellor, Mighty God, Everlasting Father, Prince of Peace, the Christ (Greek) or Messiah (Hebrew). Then the angel tells Mary, 'You will be with child and give birth to a son, and you are to give him the name Jesus' (Luke 1:31).

The names given in today's passage reflect some attributes of Jesus. They portray an image of someone far more powerful than a Christmas babe in a manger. Was there anyone ever more powerful than Jesus? Is there anything more powerful than his name today?

We sing with Salvationist songwriter Will J. Brand:

> In my heart there dwells a song of purest beauty,
> Blissful as an echo of the angel-choir must be;
> Jesus is the wondrous theme its notes are weaving;
> Dearest name of names to me.
>
> (*SASB* 70)

To ponder:

Advent gives opportunity to consider which of the myriad names for the Lord used in Scripture resonates with me. Do I use his name thoughtfully and intentionally both in prayer and in conversation?

Justice

*'Woe to those who make unjust laws, to those who issue oppressive
decrees, to deprive the poor of their rights and withhold justice from
the oppressed of my people' (vv. 1, 2).*

Israel is condemned for injustice and oppression and Isaiah keeps repeating 'his
[God's] anger is not turned away, his hand is still upraised' (9:12, 17, 21; 10:4).
Laws are meant to bring justice and defend the poor and oppressed. The laws of
many lands are founded on the Ten Commandments and biblical principles found
in the light of the New Testament. We may no longer argue 'eye for eye, tooth for
tooth' (Exodus 21:24).

The law is one thing and execution of law is another. Where there is poverty
and greed, the desire for money may overrule the truth. If a judge or a witness can
be bought there is no justice. If a government can silence those who criticise them,
they are denying free speech and may also silence truth.

If we desire goods at cheaper prices we may empower hard task-masters to
deprive the poor of their rights and to withhold justice from the oppressed. If
someone worked ten or twelve hours on Christmas Day for less than a dollar's pay,
that would be sad. Wouldn't it be even worse to realise that the underpaid person
made things that we use to celebrate Christmas? We cannot address everything,
but we are blessed by those who investigate wrongs and write about them so we
may not be ignorant, by those who tirelessly try to give information on labels so
that we can choose to shop ethically and by those who fight child trafficking.

So many people are passionate about justice, and their passion adds to our
knowledge, and our knowledge helps to change the world. We can enable them
through our prayers, resources and considerate purchases. Martin Luther King Jr
said: 'If a man hasn't discovered something that he would die for, he isn't fit to live.'

To pray:

**Lord, help me to be aware of my neighbour's situation and to treat my neighbour,
whether around the corner or around the world, with practical respect and
compassion, for your name's sake.**

Impossible

'They will neither harm nor destroy on all my holy mountain, for the earth will be full of the knowledge of the LORD as the waters cover the sea' (v. 9).

It's impossible that Father Christmas can come down the chimney: he's too big; many houses have no chimney; and, anyway, he doesn't exist! It's possible, though, that parents will give their children presents in secret and bring them great joy in the tradition of St Nicholas (Santa Claus), who helped others under cover of darkness.

In 1979 youngsters of The Salvation Army children's home in Glasgow heard bells on Christmas afternoon. They ran round the house but couldn't find the source; they ran into the garden and then saw Father Christmas behind the parapet on the roof. He had landed there and got stuck. He had a big bag of toys but no way of getting them to the children.

The chimney, while not big enough to accommodate Santa, was strong enough to hold a rope, so Father Christmas abseiled down the front of the old mansion. One little boy was opened-mouthed, with his eyes popping out of his head; another little girl was frankly fearful, with two little fingers inserted into her mouth. The traffic stopped as everyone watched the drama.

Father Christmas landed safely and duly distributed presents, and everyone started to breathe again. Whatever traumas those children had before, they subsequently had a vivid memory of a Christmas when one man put himself out to bring them pleasure.

There is hope: after all the injustice and oppression Isaiah foretells a time when a descendant of Jesse, father of David, will bring justice. At that time the impossible will be possible – the leopard will lie down with the goat. What other things are impossible? World peace? Every child in a loving home? The list could be endless, and would make a good guide for prayer.

Jesus provides the solution, both in his coming at Christmas and the words he spoke: 'With man this is impossible, but with God all things are possible' (Matthew 19:26). One day we will know a New Jerusalem, a God-centred earth: 'I am making everything new!' (Revelation 21:5).

Remnant

*'In that day the LORD will reach out his hand a second time to
reclaim the remnant that is left of his people' (v. 11a).*

Family is important. Christmas is a time to be together. Those without family,
those who are part of divorced or separated families, or families riven by
tension, deal with it in different ways. Some drown their sorrows in drink. Some
put energy into helping others: driving people to a community meal, delivering
meals or cooking them. Others who know joy and unity in the family invite
friends to share with them, although they have to respect the fact that sharing in
another's happy family may cause some people more distress than working out
their own solutions.

Family was an important factor for the Saviour of the World. Matthew 1:1–16
gives the genealogy of Christ from Abraham, through Jesse and David to Joseph,
husband of Mary, mother of Jesus. Because Joseph was of the house and line of
David he had to travel to Bethlehem for the census ordered by Caesar Augustus,
causing Jesus to be born there. Jesus came to reclaim the remnant, those left of
God's people, and bring them and others not of the faith into a life-changing
relationship with God.

Many people are finding faith today as the gospel is preached in different ways
to different people. It is the same gospel, but one person responds to the theme of
justice, another to strong rhythms which touch the soul, another to environmental
teachings respecting God the Creator and yet another to the order of liturgy. What
is sad is when part of the family feels they are the 'remnant', the part left behind in
a seemingly irrelevant religion.

Christmas is a time for sharing, and as we share what is important we will
surely find a lot of common ground, even with those who do not yet know Christ.

To pray:

> Help us to build each other up,
> Our little stock improve;
> Increase our faith, confirm our hope,
> And perfect us in love.
> *Charles Wesley*

117

The Surprise

*'But Mary treasured up all these things and pondered
them in her heart' (v. 19).*

Think of the animals found in the stable,
All bedded and warm for the night,
Suddenly stirred by a baby's crying;
What a surprising sight!
There in the manger a new Child sleeping
Under the star-studded night.

Think of a silence that's quite unsuspecting
Of what the next moment would bring,
Suddenly broken by angels singing;
What a surprising thing!
There in the silence a song was saying:
This Child our true peace would bring.

Think of a heart that has heard the same story
So often repeated before,
Suddenly catching a glimpse of its meaning;
What a surprising thing!
Joy that could not until now be imagined,
No one could ask for more!

And here for a moment again today,
In the midst of all you must do,
Let the surprise catch your heart once more,
Making the old story new.

Joy Webb

Joy

*'Gladness and joy will overtake them, and sorrow
and sighing will flee away' (v. 10).*

Home of Joy in Uganda is for children with disabilities. William has no feet but runs around on what remains of his heels, which gives him the gait of an agile person on stilts. With a ready smile he runs to open the gates for a car. He is always quicker on his stumps than in shoes. Imagine our delight, our pride when William was chosen as goalkeeper for a local football team. Isaiah 35:6 says: 'Then will the lame leap like a deer.' Every time William saves a goal he is fulfilling Scripture.

The first time I visited Home of Joy I was numb, on the second visit I was shocked, and on the third visit I was able to see some things which could be done. It is a number of years now since the oven was repaired with cow dung!

Many will still see this as a desolate place, misnamed as Home of Joy, but 'water will gush forth in the wilderness and streams in desert' (v. 6). However hot the ground to William's stumps, there is always a spring bursting forth in the grounds and supplying a constant flow of water for all the children. It knows no bounds and seems not to contain itself in the pipe people have prescribed.

This passage, titled 'Joy of the Redeemed' in the *NIV*, began to be fulfilled with the birth, life and resurrection of Jesus as he healed the sick and showed us the 'Way of Holiness' (v. 8). But it isn't just for the rescued children at Home of Joy; it's for each one of us to fulfil and bring the kingdom of God a bit nearer. One sign of this is the crocus bursting into bloom (v. 1): as a symbolic act we can plant a crocus.

Salvation Army songwriter Albert Orsborn wrote:

> O for the time of Christ's completed mission!
> Throbs of its rapture reach us as we pray;
> Gleams of its glory bursting on our vision
> Speed us to labour, urge us on our way.
> Jesus shall conquer, lift up the strain!
> Evil shall perish and righteousness shall reign.
> (*SASB* 173)

Amen!

Pathway

'A voice of one calling: "In the desert prepare the way for the LORD; make straight in the wilderness a highway for our God"' (v. 3).

One of G. K. Chesterton's poems describes the circuitous roads of England and how they were made. However, amid all these there are a number of old roads that go directly from A to B, and these are the legacy of Roman conquerors. In Uganda the roads go purposefully from A to B but then get sidetracked by heavy rains which cause so much damage that many drivers will elect to career alongside them, rather than on them. Potholes or craters also reroute the cars, which leads to the practice of driving on the left or the right or in the middle of the road depending on the most even course.

We know the Israelites wandered for many years in the wilderness. Biblical maps show their long route round the desert and then the confused meanderings at the end (very near Bethlehem where Jesus was born). Here we read of a strong voice calling to make a straight way through the desert for God himself. He will lead us home.

The figurative use of a 'pathway' or 'road' is applied frequently to our spiritual journey. Sometimes we travel directly and at other times we go round in circles. Sometimes the path is hard and uphill and sometimes we come to the crossroads of decision.

We often link these verses with the mission of John the Baptist preparing the way for Jesus. Verse 9 brings our seasonal 'good tidings' and verse 11 reflects Jesus our Shepherd.

We too need to prepare the way for Jesus to come. Some of this will involve the practicalities of celebrating Christmas, and some – more importantly – the preparation of our hearts to receive Jesus Christ once again. Graham Kendrick, the writer of many contemporary worship songs, urges us:

> Make way, make way, for Christ the King in splendour arrives.
> Fling wide the gates and welcome him into your lives.[11]

———————

To ponder:

How can I ensure that my heart is as ready as my home for Christmas, the mass of Christ, this season?

Holding Hands

'I, the LORD, have called you in righteousness; I will take hold of your hand. I will keep you and will make you to be a covenant for the people and a light for the Gentiles' (v. 6).

There is security when a mother holds her child's hand and keeps him or her safe in traffic, or is the reassuring presence which physically says, 'I am here, don't be afraid.' In some countries it is quite acceptable for adults to hold hands. In African countries, adults have held my hand and led me across the road. The first time I was surprised, but have become assured by the grasp. God the Father, Creator of hands, says, 'I will take hold of your hand' (v. 6). Although it is not immediately obvious whose hand he will take, I hope it is mine.

Scholars tell us that these verses were intended for the Israelites: to be a light for the Gentiles, or to bring salvation to everybody. The Israelites did not fulfil this role, but Jesus did, and so these verses are quoted in reference to his ministry (see Matthew 12:17–21). Jesus perfectly fulfilled this prophecy.

It is impossible to read today's passage in the abstract. Using our key verse, none of us can say the Lord does not call us to righteousness – he does. We would be foolish to say he will not hold our hand – he is with us through thick and thin. We cannot say he will not keep us, nor make covenant with us. We cannot deny him the power to use us as 'a light for the nations' (*The African Bible*).

So if our hearts aspire to follow the model Jesus gave us, we can stand prepared (albeit trembling) for the Lord's blessing found in verse 1: 'Here is my servant, whom I uphold, my chosen one in whom I delight.' If this is too awesome to consider, know that the hand of Jesus reaches out just now.

To ponder:

> What though the treacherous road may wind,
> Faith in my heart assures my mind;
> E'en when his face I do not see,
> The hand of Jesus reaches me.
>
> *Olive Holbrook (SASB 176)*

New Jerusalem

*'I will rejoice over Jerusalem and take delight in my people; the sound of
weeping and of crying will be heard in it no more' (v. 19).*

It is Christmas Eve, when we can sit serenely waiting for the Christ-child or run
round in one mad rush. Many will plan to take the children to a crib service,
celebrate Midnight Mass or go carol-singing for those who would otherwise be
alone on Christmas Eve or unable to attend church. Others will celebrate in the
best way they know how, but miss the essence of what makes Christmas special.

As traditions vary, some will hang stockings for the children, others put out
their shoes; some will have great hopes for the pillowcases and others will go to
bed hungry, with no thoughts of presents, just wondering about the next meal. It
may be hard to remember it is Christmas if you are without food and without
hope. We may share mince pies, and stare at the skies to see a special star. We want
to feel that tonight will be a special night.

The biblical story starts in the Garden of Eden, and soon things go very wrong.
Isaiah looks beyond the restored Jerusalem to a new heaven and earth, something
better than Eden or our best dreams. Today children will be hoping and dreaming
about tomorrow. As Christians we are travelling toward a heaven that many have
tried to describe, but with all the richness of our vocabulary and our imagination
we have no words or thoughts big enough.

The start of this New Jerusalem is found in the baby born in Bethlehem who
later died and was raised to life on the third day. The Prince of Peace is pivotal to
our world as we know it, and as it will become.

The carol by Edmund Hamilton Sears includes this verse:

> For lo! The days are hast'ning on, by prophet bards foretold,
> When with the ever-circling years comes round the age of gold,
> When peace shall over all the earth its ancient splendours fling,
> And the whole world give back the song which now the angels sing.

Come

'Arise, shine, for your light has come, and the glory of the
Lord rises upon you' (v. 1).

Christmas joy comes in the anticipation and preparation. We plan ahead so that those we love will be happy with the arrangements and pleased with the presents. Even when the size, colour or version is wrong, the recipients will smile, knowing an effort was made to make them happy.

We've reached the day itself. We hope the festive meal goes according to plan, and the presents bring smiles and absorption as people try on clothes, fit batteries or struggle with instructions. We might attend a simple church service, or be part of the glory of music ascending to the heights in a cathedral. Christmas Day has arrived!

The prophet says, 'Your light has come' (v. 1). He is speaking in pictures. The light can be seen as fulfilled in Christ. The blessing of the Israelites is seen in earthly terms. We look more widely to a gospel that encompasses all nations and cultures and calls them to their best. People will bring their wealth: their silver, gold and incense, some on camels and others in ships; but most important of all the people come.

We like it when family and friends send presents at Christmas, but most of all we like it when they themselves can come. Our churches like our offerings, but most of all the church fellowship likes it when we come. The shepherds, and later the magi (with their presents) come to Jesus. We look forward to the day when we are all one, all together in the New Jerusalem when 'the Spirit and the bride say, "Come!"' (Revelation 22:17).

———————

To pray:

For 'journeying mercies' for loved ones who come to share Christmas; for the people who come to join our Christmas services; for those who are close in spirit but living and working in other lands; for those for whom we have prayed will one day return to the Lord; for the coming of Jesus.

'Come, thou long-expected Jesus, born to set thy people free; from our fears and sins release us, let us find our rest in thee.'

Charles Wesley

Delight

'I delight greatly in the LORD; my soul rejoices in my God. For he has clothed me with garments of salvation and arrayed me in a robe of righteousness' (v. 10).

The day after Christmas takes various forms for different people. Many will claim it as a day of rest after serving others on Christmas Day. Some will relieve those who worked at Christmas, and take their turn where needed. Others will take the opportunity for a long walk to balance Christmas indulgence, or will write 'thank you' letters, relax in front of the television or visit relatives.

For each of us this day will take a different form. Our challenge is not to let the light of yesterday die like a damp squib but to take the glory of that celebration and continue it into reflective delight.

The Living Lord speaks to us through this passage. Jesus claimed the first two verses in Luke 4:18–19 and affirmed his purpose. He was sent not just to be the focus of nativity plays but to change the world: he is our Saviour, our salvation.

The baby in the manger grew to be the man, the human face of God, to whom many of us relate because he experienced the same joys, temptations, satisfaction, frustrations and tiredness that we experience. We can have pleasure in his service. We can delight in his will.

William Chatterton Dix emphasises the personal gladness and joy of the wise men in his carol:

> As with gladness men of old
> Did the guiding star behold,
> As with joy they hailed its light,
> Leading onward, beaming bright,
> So, most gracious Lord, may we
> Ever more be led to thee.

To ponder and pray:

Personalise the first part of today's key verse. The challenge is to complete a long list of appreciation and make this the focus of our prayers, then conclude by saying: 'LORD, you are my delight; enfold me in your reflection as I marvel in your will. Amen.'

The Man

'The true light that gives light to every man was coming into the world' (v. 9).

Born into poverty,
Far from his home;
Cradled in crudity,
Far from a throne;
And in the heart of this small helpless thing
Rested God's promise of Saviour and King

Lived in obscurity,
Often alone;
No clear identity,
Not widely known;
And in the heart of this young growing boy
Rested the promise of love, peace and joy.

Preached to the multitude,
Talked to the crowd;
Prayed in the solitude,
Rev'rently bowed;
And in the heart of this God-loving man
Rested the key to a God-ordained plan.

Model of fortitude,
Patient and kind;
Gracious in attitude,
Humble in mind;
And in the heart of this popular friend
Rested a promise that waiting would end.

Totally good and true,
God's only Son;
Hung on a cross of wood,
Life's mission done;
And in the heart of this crucified man
Rests the completion of what he began.

Out from the darkened grave,
Living and free;
Risen to help and save,
Living for me;
And in the heart of the glorified Lord
Rests lasting hope for a desperate world.

Keith Banks

A Backward Glance

We finish the year by returning to Matthew's Gospel and with a backward glance at the first four chapters. Right from the start we see Jesus identifying with those he came to save.

In response we might ask ourselves, in the words of a song from the Salvation Army musical, *Spirit*:

> For Jesus' sake, for Jesus' sake,
> What will you do for Jesus' sake?
> What will you dare, what will you bear for Jesus' sake?
> For Jesus' sake, for Jesus' sake,
> Not for yourself, not even for the sake of those you love,
> What will you risk, what will you stake,
> What will you give, what will you take,
> For Jesus' sake, for Jesus' sake?
>
> *John Gowans*

It's a strong challenge for a new year!

Whose Son?

'Joseph son of David, do not be afraid to take Mary home as your wife, because what is conceived in her is from the Holy Spirit. She will give birth to a son, and you are to give him the name Jesus, because he will save his people from their sins' (vv. 20, 21).

Matthew 1:1 states at the outset that Jesus Christ is the son of David and the son of Abraham. Matthew wrote for Jews and knew that the family tree mattered a great deal. If Jesus was the Christ, the fulfilment of the Davidic and Abrahamic covenants, he would have to be of the right lineage.

The genealogy starts with Abraham and continues in a pattern of naming the men and the sons they fathered. A few of the sons' mothers – Tamar, Rahab, Ruth and the wife of Uriah (i.e. Bathsheba) – are included, possibly because Matthew wanted to emphasise God's grace or keep Jewish pride in check.

When the fifth woman is mentioned, she is introduced differently. Until then the child is noted as of the father. When Matthew mentions Mary, he says specifically 'of whom was born Jesus who is called Christ' (v. 16). Joseph is listed as Jacob's son and the husband of Mary.

There are theories about the sets of fourteen generations and who was left out, or why, in this abbreviated genealogy. Matthew knew that Jewish thought did not require every name and that the names he included were enough to make the case that Jesus was a rightful descendant of David. Jesus' right to the throne of David, to be King of the Jews, came through his legal father's (Joseph's) heritage in Solomon.

In verse 20, when an angel spoke to Joseph in a dream and reassured him that Mary's conception was from God, Joseph is addressed as 'son of David'. The angel tells Joseph the gender of Mary's child as well as the name he should give him – Jesus (the Greek form of Joshua, meaning 'the Lord saves').

At the outset, Matthew establishes Jesus' identity as the Saviour Messiah. In verse 23 he characteristically refers to Isaiah who prophesied that the Saviour would come in just this way and would be called Immanuel ('God with us').

We rejoice in God's plan for our salvation and his presence with us!

'Lesser' Miracles

'But when he heard that Archelaus was reigning in Judea in place of his father Herod, he was afraid to go there. Having been warned in a dream, he withdrew to the district of Galilee, and he went and lived in a town called Nazareth. So was fulfilled what was said through the prophets: "He will be called a Nazarene"' (vv. 22, 23).

The Magi were elated when the star they had followed for so long and for so far led them to the right location. But when they finally saw Jesus with Mary, their jubilation turned to awe as they bowed to worship him and present their offerings to him.

In the first two chapters of Matthew, God uses dreams to communicate with men. The Magi changed their route home because of the warning they received in a dream.

Joseph received this type of guidance four times surrounding the birth and infancy of Jesus. The guidance came in assurance, then in warning, again in assurance and then in another warning. Joseph's obedience to the message from an angel of the Lord each time was vital in Jesus' early life.

At Christmas we think of the miraculous birth of Christ, but many other lesser miracles attended his coming as well.

> They all were looking for a king
> To slay their foes and lift them high;
> Thou cam'st a little baby thing
> That made a woman cry.
>
> My fancied ways why should'st thou heed?
> Thou com'st down thine own secret stair;
> Com'st down to answer all my need,
> Yea, every bygone prayer.
> *George MacDonald*

To ponder:

Before the season slips away, consider some of the 'lesser' miracles that attended Christ's coming. Think about some of the simple miracles of assurance and guidance that continue to show his work in our everyday world. Praise him!

For Us

'And a voice from heaven said, "This is my Son, whom I love;
with him I am well pleased"' (v. 17).

Matthew places the family of Joseph and Mary and Jesus back in Nazareth, then skips forward about thirty years in Jesus' life. Luke fills in more about Jesus' birth and his visit to the temple at age twelve. Luke also details John the Baptist's family background. But all four Gospels report John the Baptiser's vocation.

John's preaching theme is repentance in readiness for the imminent arrival of the kingdom of heaven. (Some Gospel-writers use 'kingdom of God' for the same concept.) Soon Jesus will preach that the kingdom has come indeed (Matthew 12:28).

John preaches with the urgency of an Old Testament prophet. Even his simple clothes and food exude an intensity of devotion to his mission. He secures his coarse camel's hair garment with a leather belt as did Elijah (2 Kings 1:8). He survives on locusts and wild honey.

Matthew describes John as the fulfilment of Isaiah's prophecy of the one who would come preparing the way of the Lord. After the transfiguration Jesus reminds his disciples that the prophesied Elijah who would prepare the way for the Son of Man has already come. They then realise he is speaking of John (Matthew 17).

Many people respond to John's message, confessing their sins and showing evidence of their new intentions by being baptised. They must have wondered what John meant by someone greater who would baptise them with the Holy Spirit's fire.

When Jesus comes as a candidate for baptism, only Matthew records that John protests. Jesus didn't need to repent of sin. Yet from the start, Jesus chose to identify with sinners. The connotation of baptism is 'identifying with'. He did it for our sakes. Praise him!

In a rare glimpse of the Trinity we see Jesus emerging from the water (Luke says he is praying), the Holy Spirit coming down on him as a dove and the voice of God from heaven validating that Jesus is his beloved Son and he is pleased with him before he even begins his ministry.

———

To ponder:

What will you do for Jesus' sake?

In Spirit and in Truth

'Jesus returned to Galilee in the power of the Spirit' (Luke 4:14).

From his commissioning, Jesus was led by the Spirit into the wilderness to be tempted by the devil. What a disheartening first appointment! He went without food for forty days and was hungry. Those who know famine understand hunger's physical symptoms. Friends who escaped from Cambodia tell me that when they had to live on scarce rations of rice, they would catch dragonflies for protein.

Even his cousin John's locust and honey diet would have been preferable to no food for forty days. The devil approached Jesus in his weakened condition (he uses the same tactic with us): 'If you are the Son of God, turn stones to bread (satisfy yourself), throw yourself off the pinnacle of the temple (establish popularity in a showy way), worship me (bypass the cross for the prize of the kingdoms of the world now).'

In the garden, the serpent tempted Eve in a similar pattern. He appealed to her appetite, then her pride and a shortcut to obtaining power. Both in Eden and in the wilderness Satan used the tactic of slightly altering God's Word. He still does.

Jesus countered each of the devil's temptations with Scripture which he introduced with 'it is written'. Finally, 'Jesus said to him, "Away from me, Satan! For it is written: 'Worship the Lord your God, and serve him only'"' (Matthew 4:10). Jesus is the Truth and through truth Jesus outwitted and overcame the evil one's lies.

God endorsed Jesus from the start of his ministry. His righteousness withstood unrighteousness. Jesus was determined to do the will of God. When the devil left, angels came to minister to Jesus. They would do so again in a different setting on the night of his final struggle to do the will of God and defeat Satan (Luke 22:41–43). What Jesus did, he did to please his Father and to redeem us. His solitary victory was for us and remains effective.

As Jesus' public ministry began, few of those he encountered knew of the spiritual battles he faced and won, or of his dependence on the Father and the Spirit. As a new year dawns, let's look at Jesus and ask him to help us be like him in this aspect.

Notes

1. Kathryn Copsey, *From the Ground Up*, in paperback (BRF, 2005).
2, 3. William Barclay, *The Daily Study Bible Series: The Gospel of Matthew*, vol. 2 (St Andrew Press, Edinburgh, 1953, revised and updated by St Andrew Press, 2001).
4. Lieutenant-Colonel Marlene Chase, *Our God Comes* (Crest Books, The Salvation Army, USA, 2000).
5. © LCS Songs, a division of Lorenz Creative Services.
6. *The Daily Study Bible Series: The Letters to the Philippians, Colossians and Thessalonians* (St Andrew Press, Edinburgh, 1959; Westminster Press, Philadelphia, Pennsylvania Revised Edition, 1975).
7. Robert Street, *Servant Leadership*, © 2003 The Salvation Army.
8. Michael Card, *Scribbling in Sand*, © 2002, InterVarsity Press, Downers Grove, Illinois, USA; Leicester, England, UK.
9. Robert Street, *Called to be God's People* (The Salvation Army's International Spiritual Life Commission – its report, implications and challenges), © 1999 The General of The Salvation Army (reprinted 2001, 2008).
10. 'The Stable Door' in *Christmas Praise*, © The General of The Salvation Army.
11. Graham Kendrick, 'Make way', © Kingsway's Thankyou Music, Eastbourne, UK.

Index

Matthew	1–4	September–December 2009
	5–10	January–April 2009
	11–18	May–August 2009
	19–20	September–December 2009
	22	September–December 2009
	24–26	September–December 2009
Luke	1–2	September–December 2005
	7–9	May–August 2004
	9–12	September–December 2004
	13–16	January–April 2005
	17–21	September–December 2005
	22–24	January–April 2006
John	1–7	May–August 2006
	3:16	January–April 2005
	8–14	September–December 2006
	15–21	January–April 2007
Acts	13–17:15	May–August 2004
	17:16–21:16	May–August 2005
	21:17–26	May–August 2006
	27–28	January–April 2007
Romans		May–August 2007
1 Corinthians	1–16	January–April 2008
	13	September–December 2005
2 Corinthians	5:17	January–April 2006
Ephesians		September–December 2008
Colossians		September–December 2009
1 Thessalonians		September–December 2005
2 Thessalonians		January–April 2006
2 Timothy		September–December 2004
Titus		May–August 2006
Philemon		May–August 2005
Hebrews		May–August 2008
		May–August 2009
James		January–April 2009
		May–August 2008
1 Peter		September–December 2008
2 Peter		January–April 2007
2, 3 John		September–December 2006
Jude		September–December 2009
Revelation	1–3	May–August 2005

Subscribe...

Words of Life is published three times a year:
January–April, May–August and September–December

Four easy ways to subscribe

- By post – simply complete and return the subscription form below
- By phone – +44 (0)1933 445 445
- By email – mail_order@sp-s.co.uk
- Or visit your local Christian bookshop

SUBSCRIPTION FORM

Name (Miss, Mrs, Ms, Mr)..

Address ....

....

.... Postcode ....

Tel. No..

Email* ....

Annual Subscription Rates
UK £10.50   *Non-UK* £10.50 + £3.90 P&P = **£14.40**
Please send me .... copy/copies of the next three issues of *Words of Life* commencing with **January 2010**

Total: £ .... I enclose payment by cheque ☐
Please make cheques payable to *The Salvation Army*

Please debit my Access/Mastercard/Visa/American Express/Switch card

Card No. ☐☐☐☐ ☐☐☐☐ ☐☐☐☐ ☐☐☐☐ **Expiry date:** ___ /___

Security No. ☐☐☐ **Issue number (Switch only)** _____

Cardholder's signature: .... **Date:** ....

Please send this form and any cheques to: The Mail Order Department, Salvationist Publishing and Supplies, 66–78 Denington Road, Denington Industrial Estate, Wellingborough, Northamptonshire NN8 2QH, UK

☐ *We would like to keep in touch with you by placing you on our mailing list. If you would prefer not to receive correspondence from us, please tick this box. The Salvation Army does not sell or lease its mailing lists.